Life was
Perfect...
UNTIL!

LUCILLE M. GRISWOLD

INK START MEDIA
5710 W Gate City Blvd Ste K #284
Greensboro, NC 27407

Lucille M. Griswold

LOOK FOR LUCILLE'S OTHER NOVELS

Grandmother's Jewels II Life Lived in Reverse: A Memoir

My Story: Only God will be my Judge Complex Love

Generations Apart Flaming Emotions Circumstantial Widows

Our Bus Driver MR. BILL – (A Children's Book)

Nuestro Conductor del Autobus SENOR BILL
(The same Children's Book offered in Spanish)

Christmas Love

Detailed Explanation of All the Books
can be found on Lucille's Website Below:

Website - lucille-griswold.com

Life was Perfect...Until!

DEDICATION

To William and all my children, their children and all of their spouses, you all make my life worth living. Also, blessings to the three newest additions to the family - Penelope Malia Griswold, Willow Lynn McDonald, and Grace Mary Cooler. You are all the icing on my cake – and to me the icing is my favorite part!

Life was Perfect...Until!

Lucille M. Griswold

Acknowledgments

Every writer knows that it takes more to write a book than just having an author. There are always edits to be made, websites to care for, and designing a cover. None of this could have been accomplished without the superior help of Sandra L. Lewallen, Michael Lewallen, Vicky Uy and Emma Davies. Whenever problems occurred, I knew just where to turn. My sincere thank you to all of them for always being available when needed.

1

Life was perfect – until it was not! To put it mildly, you could snap your cap, especially if you were an old fuddy-duddy. You might be told to take a powder because you, fat head, were full of gobbledygook. Also, don't be in cahoots with that eager beaver either. While the era of the 1940s and 1950s was full of slang words, it was not uncommon to have fear permeate the atmosphere. People became accustomed to living with the terrors of World War II, black outs and bomb shelters. Women worked in defense plants as they took over men's jobs, and dresses were replaced by females wearing pants. Since more women were working outside the home, frozen dinners replaced home cooked meals. However, not all was gloom and doom. People did the "jitterbug" as they danced to the sound of the Big Bands, and instrumental versions of the blues, like boogie woogie and the bop, kept the population mesmerized.

Despite everything, if one were to ask, the assumption might be that people who were children in the 1940s happened to be raised during the perfect time and place. A small-town atmosphere filled everyone's hearts, many had good friends, food for most was always on the table, and it appeared that a majority of people had parents who cared. Who could ask for more in their formative years?

Three girls formed a solid friendship during this time period. They all came from Smithville, this small town that they all loved. However, there was the possibility the girls' friendship might have been considered strange for someone growing up in the 1940's class conscious society. Each child's family life was considered to be in a different status category during that time period, but the girls' friendship was real and uncaring of that fact. The streets of the small town ran parallel to one another. The middle of what was called Main Boulevard had a cluster of small businesses to include a clothes cleaning establishment, a shoemaker, a drug store, and it also was home to the public library, post office and Mrs. Gibbon's "everything" shop. There was the soda fountain store where you could get delicious ice cream sodas, newspapers, cigars, cigarettes and candy. At the upper end of town were the home/offices of the physicians, dentists and attorneys for those who could afford that type of real estate. Two streets paralleled from a triangle that housed a war memorial to honor the deceased from the First World War and some from World War II after the December 7th, 1941 bombing of Pearl Harbor, Hawaii. The third connected later towards the middle of town.

The street stuck in the middle was given the name of Center Street. Most of the homes on this street were either single family homes or duplexes, and the Grammar School and High School for the town were located at the upper end of the street. A few of the homes belonged to some attorneys and other professionals who still had lovely homes without the expensive real estate of the location on Main Boulevard.

How odd that the third street was given the name of Park Avenue which usually brought to mind the ritzy area of New York City. Members of many races lived there to include a mixture of whites, blacks (though they were called Negros at that time), and one Asian family who were called Orientals by the majority of the population as the word Asian also had yet to become the proper wording in their vocabulary. No one was offended by either of these descriptions because those were the phrases used during that time period.

Barbara Gelman lived on Main Boulevard at the upper end of town. Her father was a physician who had a home office in their elegantly styled home. He also made house calls if he thought they were necessary. This was a common occurrence during that time period. Pretty, with long dark hair and deep brown eyes, many of her features depicted her Jewish heritage with the ultimate package being one of beauty. Perhaps that is one thing the three girls had in common. They were pretty, popular with both sexes, but they were also brought up to be kind and compassionate to everyone. This especially was the feature that drew them to other people.

Mia Wagner's relatives had a German background. Her father was a young attorney who could better afford a single-family home on Center Street. He worked for a group of attorneys who had their office on Main Boulevard. Her coloring contrasted Barbara's with her beautiful short blonde hair and blue eyes.

Colleen O'Conner was as Irish as the name implied. Her father owned a convenience store on Park Avenue that carried the basics for everyone, and a bar was attached that always had patrons regardless of the time of day. The bar is what made the money for the family. O'Conner's, as it was called, was the only business on that entire street of tiny homes and churches. In the summer months, the crowd that generated outside around the bar created a camaraderie of voices that could be heard on Center Street, and the music from within the bar whiffled through the summer air. Colleen's hair was a natural deep red and curly. The shorter she wore it, the curlier it became. Now, at shoulder length, her hair was full of luscious waves. She was the apple of everyone's eye not only at school and among her friends, but she also appealed to the patrons of the convenience store and bar. Most everyone in town knew and loved her.

Had the girls not been placed in the same classroom on their first day of school, while starting kindergarten, they possibly might never have met. Because the school was not overly populated, the three girls would always be promoted together clear through to high school, and they naturally became the best of friends.

Rarely did the girls play in each other's homes. They were on the phone constantly however, and during the summer months they either gathered at the community pool or they swam in the freshwater lake. Barbara's parents, as well as Mia's parents, appeared to have a fear of the lake and would have been happy if their daughters never swam in it. Colleen, on the other hand, was raised more as a free spirit. The family feared nothing and consequently, neither did Colleen. Each girls' home was within walking distance of both the grammar and high school.

Barbara went to the Synagogue in another town that was several miles away, but it was the closet to her home. Mia's parents were Protestant, and she attended the church that was located at the upper end of Main Boulevard. Colleen was as Catholic as anyone could get without attending the Catholic Schools. The Catholic Church was located on Main Boulevard but closer to the Triangle where the War Memorial was situated and not in any way near one of the several Protestant churches.

Life seemed simple in those days. The girls could leave their home early in the day and only come home for meals later in the evening when the streetlights came on. If they packed a lunch, they could be gone all day. The mothers knew their daughters would be fed by any of the parents, so if they were not home at lunch time, and they had not made lunch for themselves that day, no one was overly concerned. Often, they would relax on someone's front porch and talk about boys – their favorite topic. Sometimes, they rode their bikes around the back roads to friends' homes who lived in those areas. For all purposes, life was great and the girls had the privilege of growing in an atmosphere that treated them well and helped them lead a good life – until!

2

Most of the mothers walked their children to school on the very first day. The school was an old two-story brick building with lots of stairs. The odor of milk permeated the hallways, as little cartons of milk were available to all children at lunch time. Oddly, for most people milk does not even have an odor, but years later that was the one thing all three girls remembered – the odor of milk. Some children were bussed in from the rural area farms, but not the three girls who lived on Main Boulevard, Center Street and Park Avenue. The schools were within easy walking distance of all three streets, so after the first day when the girls initially met each other, they gravitated to Center Street, cutting through on side streets. They all met at a particular location and walked together from there to the school.

The playground was quite different from what you see scattered throughout the United States in the 2,000's. Swings were high on metal posts that could rust over time and possibly create hazards, but the three girls never knew anyone injured on them. They were also built on cement. If you were to fall off the seat of the swing, the dire consequences were obvious. Dodge ball and leapfrog over one of the biggest boys at the school provided all with a good time at recess. The large boy never got to leapfrog over anyone, and it is a wonder his bodily posture was not affected by the bent over position. However, he had a gentle personality and never objected to be the person everyone leaped over daily.

The three girls noticed each other immediately on that first day and gravitated towards each other. The bond they formed during that time was never broken. They went through a period of wanting to wear jodhpurs, as they were all privileged to ride Barbara's horse. They also each were given a baton to learn to twirl on one of their many Christmases. Though, as the time wore on, they didn't try out for the marching band, but all tried out for the varsity cheerleading squad. One did not make it the first year they tried out, but eventually, all became cheerleaders.

They did everything together. If the school had a Variety Show, they all participated. Because they all lived in close proximity to the school, staying late was never a problem, and they often stayed late to work on the school newspaper and yearbook. It was also nice knowing they always had a friend to sit with at the cafeteria. They did not gloat at that fact. Especially on the first days of any school year they were conscious of those who appeared to be alone, and they invited those people to sit with them. People in the neighborhoods knew the girls and watched out for them as they travelled back and forth to school. Again, life appeared to be ideal – until!

* * *

Not that the girls were "goody two shoes" by any means. Having the typical streak of most children to defy their parents was part of their mixture. For example, until the incident happened that stopped a bad behavior, the girls used to tell their parents they were going to the community pool when they went to the creek where all the boys congregated instead. They were about thirteen at the time and would leave in the morning with their bathing suits under their clothes and with a lunch made by their mothers that they put in the baskets that were attached to their bikes.

Often the girls were smart enough to make an appearance at the pool just in case if anyone were asked, they could justifiably say that yes, they had seen the girls there. All kinds of dangerous things went on at the creek. Someone had attached a rubber tire to a weak limb on the branch of a tree. Especially the boys used to "show-off" their silliness by doing all sorts of weird things on that tire while it was out over the water. Eventually, they would attempt a flip and hopefully land in a part of the creak deep enough so as to not hurt themselves. In reality, it is a wonder more did not get hurt.

One part of the creek had a very rough current that most of the kids tried to avoid. If caught in the current, you might not be able to get out, and it unfortunately led to a waterfall that in itself was a danger. One day, Mia daringly rode the tire because, yes, the girls were "show-offs" too. When she dropped, she fell into the dangerous current and was swiftly being carried away. The other two girls screamed with all their might catching the attention of two older boys who were good swimmers. They both immediately dove into the current part of the creek and swam their hearts out attempting to reach Mia. Eventually, one of the boys was able to grab her arm and held on to her and the trunk of a tree that protruded in the water nearby. His friend finally reached the two of them. They both held on to Mia and the tree trunk until miraculously someone had a rope in their car and threw it out to the three of them. Somehow, the rope provided a safety harness as they wrapped it first around Mia and later around themselves. Another group of children pulled the three of them to safety. Thank God the two boys were there that day as what may have happened was just too scary to even consider.

The other two girls hugged their friend with such intensity that the hug itself nearly took her breath away. They brought her to a blanket on the ground with the sun shining on it. They laid her down upon the blanket and secretly gave thanks to their own particular God that day. Once Mia's bathing suit was completely dry, the three of them took off for home. It was a long time before they ventured back to the creek, but eventually they did go there though perhaps with more caution. Leaving the daredevil stuff to the boys, the girls were just eager to flirt with them as young teenagers often do.

Then there was the gulley. Attached to a wonderful park in the middle of town not far from Barbara's home on Main Boulevard, the gulley was almost a ludicrous feature not expected to be in existence in that beautiful little park. All manner of children gathered there to climb tree limbs that hung way over land that would have been a death-defying drop if any of the children fell. One day, two of the larger boys got in a fight while attempting to maneuver over one of the thicker limbs. The girls turned around to watch where the noise was coming from only to actually see one of the boys nicknamed "Rabbit" push the other boy off the limb. The girls were disbelieving at what they saw. They watched Roy tumble down the great abyss and they feared the worst. However, Roy got caught on a ledge instead of falling to the bottom. How many of us have similar stories to tell? Was this Divine intervention?

Coming from a medical family, Barbara knew instantly what to do since her home was so close to the park. After explaining to her friends, she ran with all her might to get her father. Since this was Saturday in the late afternoon, Barbara knew her Dad would have no patients since he only worked a half a day on Saturday in the morning. She dashed through the kitchen and went directly to her father's den/office not related to his practice which was now closed off from the home for the rest of the weekend. Her father was seated in a plush maroon leather chair in the beautiful room. The chair matched the dark wall paint with white trim on the wood surfaces. The shelves were stacked with floor to ceiling books that had a ladder on a track that slid from side to side so one could reach the books at the very top, or in the middle. He was actually reading one of the books when Barbara sped into the room.

"What brings my bright chickadee into my room running at such a fast speed?"

"Daddy, come quickly. Roy's been hurt in the park. He's caught on a ledge near the gulley."

Dr. Gelman thought to inquire what his daughter was doing near the gulley at the park, but seeing the fear on his daughter's face, he decided to instead grab his medical bag. On his way out the door, he yelled to Barbara to please write a note to her mother explaining his whereabouts, so she would not worry when she returned from shopping. Barbara did just that before speeding back to the sight of the accident.

Everyone in town knew Rabbit. He was the loner boy who slept in many different homes and was fed by anyone in whatever home he was visiting. They also knew Roy and his family. While the girls waited for Dr. Gelman, they shouted down to Roy that they were getting help and told him not to worry. His loud cries defied their reassurances, however. Mia and Colleen were contemplating what to do about the situation. If they acknowledged seeing Rabbit push Roy off the tree limb, they had to admit they were near the gulley – a place they were forbidden to go. Yet, should something drastic happen to Roy, they knew they would have to tell and take the consequences. Nevertheless, when Rabbit ran by the two remaining girls, they both yelled that they saw what he had done. By telling him, they hoped that putting the fear in him would somehow help him not to do something so drastic again.

Before leaving his home, Dr. Gelman made a quick call to some of his friends on the local volunteer fire and rescue squad. He left with the assurance that someone would be at the site quickly. When Dr. Gelman saw Roy's precarious location on the ledge, he was all the more concerned. Knowing there was no way he could get down to the ledge, he attempted to use his reassuring voice to placate Roy who had now become unusually quiet. Dr. Gelman feared Roy had become unconscious and doubly feared he might fall off the ledge. At this point, the rescue team arrived and took over, somehow managing to retrieve Roy's body off the ledge. They then put him on a stretcher and placed the stretcher on a picnic table where Dr. Gelman examined the boy. Apparently, the leg took the brunt of the fall, and it was broken, probably causing Roy to black out from so much pain. After examining Roy's head for any injuries, and the rest of his body for other signs of injury, he was confident that Roy's head had not been damaged in any way, and that the leg was the main concern. He told the rescue team that he would notify Roy's parents when he got back to his office where the team took Roy for the Doctor to properly prepare the broken leg.

Mia and Colleen went home and Barbara, who it appeared was following in her father's footsteps by heading for a medical career, assisted her father. It was not a common occurrence for women to become physicians in the 1940's, but the Gelmans were not traditional in their thoughts or actions. When Roy recovered from his stupor, Barbara listened carefully to Roy's responses to her father's questions. He never once mentioned that Rabbit had pushed him. Most likely he too was embarrassed as well because he had been playing in the gulley. The gulley was not a place most parents would enjoy having their children play. He also probably did not want to admit that the two boys were having some type of silly argument. Barbara later told her friends that she would follow Roy's actions and not mention what Rabbit had done, and she hoped her friends would follow her example. Of course, that was the easy solution, and both girls were willing to follow in their friend's footsteps.

So, some of the time, the girls lucked out and were not caught doing naughty things, but there were times when they did get caught. The punishment was always immediate and dreaded, but it kept the girls in line.

3

Prom was fast approaching. Mia and Colleen's mothers were making the gowns for their daughters. Barbara's gown came from an elegant couture shop in the closest city. Mia's mother was getting quite concerned because it took Mia so long to decide which boy, among the many who asked her, she would finally give her approval. Consequently, Mrs. Wagner could not spend as much time on the details that she desired.

The prom was scheduled during the early parts of the month of May. This was probably going to be the last big event of the school year since graduation was set for the first week in June. The girls felt privileged to have almost the entire month of June off to wile away some summer days, at least until their siblings' school days ended for the year. Barbara had a younger brother and twin sisters almost ten years younger than she was. Mia had a sister that was two years younger, and she would be entering her junior year of high school. Colleen had no siblings. This fact added to her free spirit identity.

When the weather was nice out, which during the months of April and May were most days, the girls would gather at one or the other's front porch with the intention of studying for tests and later in May for finals. Inevitably, the conversation turned more towards their dates for prom and the arrangements they were making to all go to a nightclub in the city once the prom ended. This was the customary thing to do in their area where they often got to dance to the big bands. The prom always had a live band, but it was usually local talent. This, of course, suited everyone just fine.

Mia remembered being asked to the prom when she was a junior by one of the senior guys. Her excitement diminished when they double dated with a senior couple who were to get married soon after graduation. They did nothing but "make out" in the back seat of the car both to and from prom and God knows what they managed to accomplish back there on the way to the city afterwards. The sounds coming from the back of the car and the lack of consideration for the couple in the front of the vehicle was an embarrassment to Mia. She was not hoping for a repeat.

The young woman felt better this year knowing the three of them and their dates, along with another couple, were going to the prom together. All had rented a limo that was most likely paid for by the parents. This turned out to be a blessing since if the children drank too much they would not end up behind the wheel of a car. Renting a limousine was not common practice yet for most who attended the prom, as it became many years later. Most borrowed their parents' best car for this occasion and one could see many of the young men washing the cars in the driveways of their homes during the afternoon of the prom.

The fourth couple were more friends of the boys in the group. The fourth boy attended a private school as did his date, but he was the neighbor of one of the other three boys. He had brought his date to the public school to see the senior play in which most of this group had a part, so they all had the privilege of meeting one another and got along well. All were happy to include this couple in their limo ride after the couple decided to attend this school's prom instead of their own private school.

All the girls looked beautiful, each in their own way. The homemade gowns were just as elegant as those that were pre-made from a dress shop. Barbara's gown was indeed stylish and consisted of a beige color with lots of sparkling sequins dotting the bodice of the dress which had cap sleeves. The beige color made her dark hair and brown eyes stand out even more. The mother of little blonde Mia did a superb job. The royal blue strapless dress showed off Mia's beautiful silky skinned shoulders over which she wore a matching shawl while the dress coloring also accentuated Mia's blue eyes. Colleen's pale green lace dress and fitted bodice were perfect to heighten the color of her beautiful red hair. The dress had one shoulder bare. The other side covered the opposite shoulder with a small bow and was otherwise sleeveless.

Often Mia and Colleen were called in from their playdates for a fitting, but no one ever objected. Barbara's mother helped run the office part of her Dad's practice, so when Barbara had the privilege of buying her gown at a special shop, no one appeared to object. It was not uncommon for Mrs. Wagner to help out at the local dry cleaners when necessary, but for the most part she was home all day and did a lot of sewing for her two girls. The same situation applied to Mrs. O'Conner who took a portion of every day to help out in the convenience store of their establishment so the others could take some time for lunch. She only sewed for special occasions and only for her child.

Prom night finally arrived and the children all looked transformed into something special.

* * *

During their freshman year in high school a power couple (something unusual in those days where both parents had a prominent job) moved from the big city to the small town. They brought with them one teenage daughter. Because the trio of Barbara, Mia and Colleen were so friendly they immediately accepted the new girl Margaret Chapman. Most called her Margie.

The group learned to do service work before it became popular by volunteering at the Methodist church where one of the four was a member. They were constantly making food baskets at holiday time and baby sitting in the church while the parents attended church services.

Since Barbara went to the Synagogue on Saturdays, and Colleen went to the very early Sunday Mass, it was easy for all the girls to babysit during the 11 o'clock service. Margie's family did not attend any church, so in many ways she was even more free spirited than Colleen.

While the Chapmans were not into going to church, they often went to the Saturday night movie in town where all the teens went with their dates. Mia had not yet committed herself to any one boy that freshman year, so it was often a literal fight between the two guys she was dating. One presumed he could go into the theater and seat himself next to Mia. Often it happened that seat was already occupied by the opposing fellow and one night it took all surrounding Mia to keep the two guys from killing each other.

Often, the Chapmans provided more of a show than the movie itself. They used to smooch it up like two teenagers to the embarrassment of all the teens in the theater who provided a whispering chain to make everyone aware of what was transpiring. Mrs. Chapman did have a nice figure and was not hesitant to show it off. Short shorts were in style for most of the teens during that era, but Mrs. Chapman wore them herself to show off shapely legs, and her tops were more revealing than was customary. The teen boys without dates used to make a point of sitting really close to the couple and enjoyed the show Margie's parents put on more than the show on the screen. It did not matter if the movie happened to be in the very new technicolor, or not. To sit near the Chapmans in the dark theater was to the teen boys much more rewarding.

The Chapmans had purchased a beautiful extravagant home in the country. At least the home appeared extravagant compared to all the farm homes in the area some of which still had wells where you pumped your own water. They dug themselves what was a natural swimming pool which was basically a huge hole in the ground filled with water.

One night for Margie's birthday, the three girls all were going to stay overnight at the Chapman's. The mothers of the girls were not so sure they wanted their daughters to go. When each daughter prompted that so-and- so's mother was letting her go, that rather helped them make their decision, and off the girls went. What the mothers did not know was that Mrs. Chapman was going to let the girls swim nude in the makeshift pool.

"I've never felt so unencumbered," said Barbara, as she felt as guilty as one could get.

"I know," agreed Mia, "the freedom of not wearing a swim suit and swimming in the pool is like nothing I've ever experienced before."

All Colleen could do was float around completely immersed in this new experience as she kept saying, "Oh Lord, this is great. Oh, my Lord, this is super."

The girls could have easily remained in the pool all night until they saw headlights coming up the long drive. They immediately ran out of the pool, grabbed towels and ran inside the house, giggling all the way.

It turned out to be a carload of their male friends. The boys had heard about the small party and invited themselves. Mrs. Chapman did invite them inside and told them to relax in the finished basement explaining that the girls had just come in from swimming, and they would be down in the basement area soon. The guys did not mind one little bit because the basement was filled with chips, pretzels and cookies, and they munched away to their heart's content.

The rest of the night was spent playing charades, dancing, and then the inevitable spin the bottle. Often, they would go in the closet to take their kiss and it took some a lot longer to come out over the others. Probably, a lot had to do with how much they liked where the bottle pointed.

4

Nevertheless, it was not necessary to discuss the topic of what they should say to their parents and what they should not say. The unspoken word was inherent in all three girls. Swim naked - not! Boys coming to the party - not!

When each girl arrived home at the end of that weekend, they thought they "had it in the bag" as the saying goes. Ecstatic in their telling was the beautiful home, the fun swimming pool the family dug on their own, the good food and the glorious weekend they had. Seemingly pacified, none of the parents pursued the weekend conversation any further. Each girl went to her room to finish what little homework they still had left to do and got ready for school the next day before going to bed.

However, the city parents apparently had a different set of standards. Mrs. Chapman thought that swimming in the pool naked was quite normal since there were no boys in the area. The fact that a car load of boys came by later did not bother her either. In fact, it just made things easier for her in the long run because she did not have to be concerned how to keep the girls amused. Just having the boys there kept the girls entertained automatically. Therefore, she thought nothing of talking about her weekend when she went to town on Monday.

News spread fast in the small town. There are always those who like to think the pretty girls, or nice girls, are not all that nice, and they will do anything to try and ruin their reputation.

Soon, the mothers of the three girls heard what happened. Either a gossipy friend called them on the party line phone, or they heard the news over the back fence, but hear it they did. By the time the girls got home from school, the mothers were fuming.

Time out was not so much in fashion in those days. Just hearing a parent raise their voice to tell them how upset they were and the shame they brought to the family was enough to make the girls cringe. Instinct told them to promise to never to do anything like that again.

Everyone that is except Colleen. Her Irish blood said what she did was not bad at all and she let her parents know it, and a big fight ensued. "There were not boys around when we went swimming, so we did nothing wrong."

The father explained in an extremely harsh tone, "Nice girls don't go swimming in the nude," and he winced even saying the word.

"What's wrong in not wearing a bathing suit in the dark water at night when no one can see you?"

"Proper ladies don't do things like that," said the mother.

"Well then I guess I am not a proper lady, whatever the heck that is."

"Watch your tone of voice young lady when you talk to your mother."

"I have thoughts too Daddy, and you should hear my side of the story also."

"In our eyes, what you did was wrong, and you did not tell us boys were coming to the party."

Colleen's shoulders dropped in desperation when she replied, "I DID NOT KNOW THE BOYS WERE COMING," just as loud as she could.

"HOW CAN YOU BLAME ME FOR SOMETHING THAT I DID NOT KNOW WAS GOING TO HAPPEN?"

Mrs. O'Conner yelled back, "Keep your voice down. Don't you ever use that tone of voice with us again. You have shamed our family and ruined your reputation."

In desperation, Colleen looked at both of her parents and realizing the conversation was going no place, she ran up to her room in tears.

The mother and the father looked at each other and momentarily were at a loss for words. Mrs. O'Conner sat on a kitchen chair and put her arms on the kitchen table with her head in her hands in sheer frustration.

The Dad went over to her and put his arms around her. "Maybe we spoke too harshly to Colleen."

"She's embarrassed this family terribly. Maybe we were not harsh enough."

"Stop and think about it honey. We're embarrassed because of our feelings of what others are thinking of us. We are not really thinking about Colleen. She's right. How can we blame her for something about which she was unaware? We are thinking more of our own selves and what people might think of us. Not about our child."

For a long time, Mrs. O'Connor just sat there with her head in her hands. She didn't say a word. Then, she started shaking her head up and down to indicate her husband was correct before she said, "You are right! I was thinking more of the hurt to us rather than thinking really about the situation. In fact, I bet it felt darn good swimming without anything on your body to encumber you. And, if she did not expect those boys to come, how can we blame her for that?

Mr. O'Connor smiled at his wife when she mentioned swimming without clothes. He bent down to kiss her and said, "Why don't we go up and take off our clothes and experience the feeling."

The mother did not complain and offered her husband a kiss as she followed him up the stairs. She whispered to him as they climbed the stairs, "This too shall pass. The gossips will be on to something else tomorrow."

They first knocked on Colleen's door. When she told them to come in, they went in and embraced their daughter while telling her they were sorry they reacted the way they did. That evening all turned out well in the O'Conner household.

At Mia's house, her father the attorney handled the situation as though she were a client with his questions. In the end, they asked Mia in the future to think of how something may appear before actually indulging. Mia knew they were angry nevertheless and apologized for her actions. She did not like disobeying her parents, and when she kept the information quiet by not telling them, she already knew that they were not going to like what happened. This was especially true knowing the reputation of the city couple.

There was a little fight going on at Barbara's home with both sides getting momentarily angry at one another. Before bedtime however, they too resolved the issue in their own way, and prayed it would all go away the next day.

5

While volunteering took up a lot of their time, in the evening sometimes the three girls would babysit for young couples who had children and wanted a night out. Usually, the people who knew them best chose them which usually meant that if you lived at the upper end of Main Boulevard, the couples who lived there chose Barbara. The same applied to those who lived on Center Street and Park Avenue. They chose the girls they knew the best.

Consequently, they lived in close proximity to the people where they babysat. So, it was not necessary to drive the girls to their home. The parents either stood at their opened door, or on their front porches and watched the girls walk home making sure they got inside. The final indication they were home was when they waved to each other that they were home and going inside.

It was as much a treat for the children as it was for the parents. All three girls enjoyed babysitting. To think they would get paid at the end of the evening for having so much fun was an added plus. Usually, the children had been fed their dinner and were allowed a snack after. This meant the girls got a snack too. They had open access to the refrigerators and enjoyed the many goodies that were inside. Sometimes, if the family had any boys, they often developed a crush on the sitter and would become all giddy and silly just at the mention of their name.

The girls really did not need money for anything in those days which meant their bank accounts were growing. Each stacked away most of the cash in the bank with the exception of a few dollars to buy a coke or ice cream soda at the local soda fountain that also was a meeting place. It was there that the guys looked for the girls and vice versa.

One day Barbara got a phone call from her close neighbor asking if she could babysit. Barbara had a family birthday party to attend on the requested evening and felt terrible having to refuse. The lady asked if Barbara knew of anyone else that might be able to do it. Barbara gave her the phone numbers of Mia and Colleen.

The neighbor tried Colleen first and she sounded great, and she also had the time they requested available. Because of the distance involved, and the late hour they might get home, the husband picked up Colleen and when the evening was over, he was going to take her home.

The children were fascinated by Colleen's beautiful red hair and her sweet face, and they instantly adored her. Her bubbly personality fit the children's just fine, and the evening, up to that point, was a success. The children even went to bed without a problem and were fast asleep by the time their parents returned. After the parents got home and both sides finished talking about the evening and what they had done, the husband left with Colleen.

He was a nice-looking young father who had this great personality, so what happened next was totally unexpected. They were riding along slowly enjoying small chit chat when the guy removed his right hand from the steering wheel and rubbed it over Colleen's breast. At first, she was so innocent she thought perhaps a bug had landed on her and the neighbor was swatting it away. As the hand rubbed more fully over the same area, Colleen grabbed his arm and removed it with defiance screaming for him to keep his hands to himself and to never touch her again.

Colleen's reaction startled the neighbor, so he did what he was told.

Somehow, he was not expecting such a reaction from this young red headed beauty, as he weirdly expected her to be more the wild type. However, he sadly misinterpreted everything about her and her looks. Colleen may have looked like a flirtatious beauty, but her upbringing defied the look she presented, and she was a good girl especially in her moral background. Anyway, by that time they were home. Colleen jumped out of the car without saying a word and slammed the car door.

Once inside her home, the parents were anxious to hear all about her evening. Colleen tried to be her usual ebullient self, and while she told about the cute children and the great evening, she never mentioned anything about coming home in the car. Oddly, she felt that if she did so, her parents and the man's wife especially might have thought she was the one to provoke the situation. She went to bed that night upset wondering what the heck she should do, if anything.

When she awoke the next morning, she did not feel any better. Monday, on her way to school, she met her friends at the usual place and accompanied them the rest of the way. Barbara started talking about the baby-sitting job and Colleen tried her best not to show any remorse. By now, Colleen had made up her mind she was not going to bring the subject up again. The parents of the children were well adored by their neighbors as well as respected. How can I tell what happened? Who is going to believe a teenage girl over a respected married couple? While most things in life she shared with her friends, this was a time she would not share.

Barbara seriously said, "I'm jealous Colleen. I really do think the children like you the best of any babysitter they ever had."

"You are being kind Barbara. They only like me because I was new to them and we did have fun, so they associate that experience as a perpetual one. Of course, that was a rare experience, and the next time all of us could be in a mood that is not at all flattering.

"Oh, no I'm not," reiterated Barbara. "Even the parents said they would definitely ask you to babysit again."

"Well, how nice of them to say that, but I'm sure you Barbara are still the apple of their eye. You guys do anything exciting over the weekend? Changing the subject seemed the proper thing to do but keeping it out of her mind was quite another. It was hard to keep this secret from her best friends or from her parents. On some occasions, Colleen saw the couple around town, and that did not help.

Apparently, the Gelman's neighbor had second thoughts about what he did as well realizing he really misinterpreted the beautiful girl's personality. He should have known better realizing she was a personal friend of Barbara's and knowing the standards Barbara's parents had set for her.

 However, he did hear rumors that those three girls were swimming in the nude at some country setting. Typically, he knew not where or when, or if what he heard happened to be really true. Just looking at the young beauty set his mind in turmoil though. He worried himself sick about how long it would take for Colleen to reveal what he did. He also wondered how soon his wife was going to hear the news.

Several weeks had gone by, and one day Barbara's neighbors called Colleen's house to see if she could babysit. Mrs. O'Connor took the message and promised to relay it to her daughter when she got home from school while also saying the calendar showed Colleen to be free that night, so it should not be a problem.

* * *

As soon as Colleen got home from school, her mother gave her the message while also stating, "I told her it would not be a problem because the calendar showed you were free that night."

Colleen was on her way upstairs and upon hearing her mother utter those last words, she abruptly turned around and uncharacteristically raised her voice when she said, "Why did you speak for me? You had no right to do that mom. I don't want to babysit for them on that night."

"Well, why? You have nothing marked on your calendar."

"Maybe I just don't want to, and you should never speak for me. I can make up my own mind."

"Excuse me? You are not allowed to go any place without our permission, not even to babysit. So, when we do approve, and it is a good way for you to earn money, I think we should know a reason if you choose not to go there."

Colleen realized her reaction might create more suspicion, so she tried to tame her response by saying, "The children really liked me Ma, maybe more so than they did Barbara, and the whole situation is awkward. I don't want them to get used to calling me."

Mrs. O'Connor sat down at the kitchen table where she was about to drink a cup of hot tea. Colleen noticed the plate of sliced lemons and took them off the counter placing them near her mother. After contemplating her answer and seeing that her daughter was visibly upset, she quietly said, "I think I understand your situation. You will need to call them nevertheless and just tell them you are sorry your mother thought you were not busy, but you are, and you just did not mark your calendar. Next time watch your anger though, and don't take it out on me. I had no idea of this situation."

Colleen went to her mother and kissed her neck. "I'm sorry Ma. I'll try never to do that again." She poured herself a cup of tea, grabbed a cookie out of the cookie jar, and the mother and daughter sat for a while together discussing other issues involving her father's business. Some men got into a fight after leaving the bar the other night and the police arrested them.

"Do we know who they were Ma?"

"No, fortunately they were from out of town. The police put them in jail for one night and told them never to come back. I hope they listen. Around here we know most of the town drunks. Usually, before anyone has to call the cops, someone familiar will take care of the situation before it escalates. That is the last thing we need is to have the police coming around our establishment, with the exception of those policemen who are customers. It will give us a bad reputation."

"Don't worry Ma. It's probably just a one-time thing. Everybody loves this small town and wants to keep it pleasant and not confrontational."

A few times Colleen did see the man who drove her home out in the town with his family. It helped that she was walking down the other side of the street, and they all could wave at each other as they passed.

One Saturday, she was at the public library browsing through the books on the shelf. Someone came up behind her and she jumped because she was not expecting anyone in such close proximity.

She was shocked when the father of the little children actually apologized to her saying, "I'm sorry Colleen for what I did to you when taking you home that night. Those actions were completely out of the ordinary for me. I do want to thank you for not telling anyone. It saved us both not having to explain ourselves."

Colleen was fearful and actually stepped away from him, but she did say, "Just don't let it happen again," with a demeanor that told him to 'lay off' her in the future, and that she "preferred if they never call her again to babysit."

He surprisingly said, "Well, that's a shame because the children actually adored having you as their sitter, but I'll tell my wife I saw you today. I'll also tell her you are more busy than usual and therefore are removing your name from any new babysitting projects." At that he walked away.

Standing there dumbfounded, Colleen could not believe he actually apologized. She took his statement for what it was worth and hoped she would never hear from anyone in that family again. Was he acting normally? She did not know. The only thing Colleen did know was that he essentially, to her amazement, never bothered her again.

6

Most of their days went by without incident. In fact, the things already mentioned were about as bad as they could get. Not that the girls never fought with one another because they did. What then happened it created a lot of snubbing, talking to the one remaining friend to get her perhaps to agree that the third one was just wrong. It was always wise not to take sides because fights did not last long, and if you got yourself involved after the fact, the others might then turn on you.

One of the hardest things that sort of affected all the girls was when Colleen's dad traveled to the mid-west to care for a sick father. No one knew how long he would be gone. Both Colleen and her mom took it very hard. Her mother's brother could easily take over running the bar with the help that was available, so they did not expect a problem there. It did mean that Mrs. O'Conner would have to work full time at the convenience store, but Colleen was old enough now and could be left on her own. Colleen's knowledge of how to work the store's cash register did come in handy though. When she was needed, it was a big help to her mother to realize how capable she was when working in the store.

Colleen and her mother's eyes were filled with tears though they tried their best to be brave. Mr. O'Conner was bursting with all kinds of emotions. He was certainly sad. For one thing, he had no idea how long he would be gone. He also did not know what to expect when he got to his father's house. Yet, the hardest thing of all was he knew it would be best if he did not show his emotions. He instead wanted to depict an aura of bravery and strength for his family.

Jack was born on the east coast and remained with friends of the family to finish school when his parents decided to go west. They had heard of a new development in Missouri. Being adventurous, they agreed to leave their only son behind because they had heard that during that time no school existed where they were going. The object was to send for their son once they had a school he could attend. The day they left was the last time Jack had seen his mother and father in years. The school in the west near the parents' home never materialized. Upon graduation, Jack married Doris and together they purchased the store and bar on Park Avenue.

This was to be the first time Jack had ever been away from his family that he dearly loved. The long ride by car was also a first, and Jack took it with great trepidation. He spent his last few minutes before he left repeating what the women needed to do. Doris assured her spouse that since her brother was actually retired now and his wife had died, he was more than willing to take over while Jack was gone.

Jack had finished putting his suitcases in the trunk of the car. Colleen could no longer hold back her tears as they filled her beautiful eyes and ran down her cheeks. The father grabbed his daughter and held her close as he kept repeating, "I know honey, I know. It's going to be all right. I'll be back before you know it." Doris stepped forward, and for a short time the father pulled both mother and daughter to his body and gave them each a big hug. Colleen finally pulled herself away so the father could grab the mother and give her the hug and kiss she deserved. Starting to close the trunk and get in the car, Jack realized his wife was still holding the bag of goodies in her hand that also included his lunch. He jokingly grabbed the bag away from Doris and put in on the front seat of the passenger side. The trip was going to be a long one. They put their hands against the window pane of the car almost willing it not to go any further as the father attempted to drive away. He touched his palms against theirs with the window in between. They stayed that way momentarily until the car finally pulled away from the house. That day Colleen matured a lot all in a few hours. The two women stood watching the car until it became a tiny speck and then disappeared completely. The two females walked back in to the house while wondering how they would ever manage with their father gone.

* * *

For some reason, all the father wanted to do was focus on his sadness, but the distractions of driving finally settled his mood. While it was still daylight, Jack enjoyed looking out the window at the countryside watching it go from a small-town atmosphere to the city buildings high and crowded together and eventually to pastures with cows and horses. He wished he could be taking this trip more for pleasure with his family along. All of the United States were beautiful, each in their own way, and Jack wanted to document and express his thoughts to his wife and daughter, but of course that was not going to happen. He promised himself to keep a mental ledger. Once in Missouri, he would document what he had seen by writing letters home.

The western part of Missouri, during the time Jack's parents decided to move to the state, was close to the Dust Bowl and suffered the drought and other conditions that created the Dust Bowl situation of states further west. Not all parts of Missouri suffered the same fate however. Bagnell Dam was built in the early 1930's that created a lot of jobs, so while the western part of the state was suffering, the central part of the state did well during the Great Depression. President Roosevelt's New Deal and his Works Progress Administration (WPA) also created jobs and was one of the reasons besides their adventuresome spirit the O'Conners decided to move there.

The trip for Jack took several days. Some evenings he was lucky to find an inexpensive place to stay. Other nights, Jack pulled off the road to a seemingly safe area and slept in his car. Each day he would check the map he brought with him, so that finally when he arrived to his parents' home in Missouri he was at once filled with excitement as well as fear concerning the condition of his father. Jack had given his mother an estimated time of arrival from his house phone before he began the trip west. Once that day arrived, the elderly Mrs. O'Conner constantly peeked through her living room curtains in anticipation of Jack's arrival.

The closer Jack got to his home, the more excitement he felt, both good and bad. He was naturally thrilled to see his mother and father whom he had not seen in years, but he was also extremely fearful of finding out the state of his father's health. Finally, the day came, as Jack turned down Daffodil Lane. He could not help but notice that all the streets were named after flowers in this housing section. When he saw his parents' house number and turned into their drive, Jack could barely contain himself. It was a simple brick ranch house, but the home was well kept, and the lawn had recently been mowed. The landscaping provided an aura of precision and peace as though nothing could be wrong in that house. He wondered who had cut the grass since he knew his mother was kept busy tending to the father. Jack had stopped at a gas station rest room to freshen himself just minutes before arriving at the house. As he exited the car and went to the trunk to retrieve his luggage, he noticed the curtains moving on his way into the house as though someone were peeking through them. The front door opened and out walked this beautiful woman with a head full of gray hair. The smile on her face could not have been bigger. A sweet voice inquired, "Jack?" Jack placed his suitcases on the ground and ran the rest of the way, picking his mother up in the air while twirling her around in circles, and he gave her the biggest hug ever.

"Oh, my goodness, is this the child we left back east so many years ago? The face is just as handsome, but you are no longer that scrawny boy that we left behind. You have matured to a full-grown man with muscles, and a sturdy stature I strangely was not expecting. But of course, this would be so." By this time Jack had put his mother back down on the ground and Cora, while still holding Jack, held him an arm's length away saying, "Let me look at you child."

Jack just stood their smiling at his mother. She finally said, "Beautiful," before releasing Jack and ushering him to the house. The living room was well put together and the décor barely looked used. Off to the right was a bedroom where she told Jack he would be sleeping, and that is where he deposited his belongings on the floor. As he returned to the living room, his mother asked him if he wanted something to eat. "I'm not hungry yet, but I sure would like a cold beer."

"Come with me to the kitchen and sit at the table a few minutes before I take you to see your father. I want to explain a few things to you. Neither of us drink any alcoholic beverages, but I did buy beer just for you as I remembered you owned a bar and store."

"Thanks Ma. It hits the spot."

Cora went on to explain Jim's condition. She expressed that it was some form of tuberculosis that destroyed the frame of the man.

"What is this thing called tuberculosis Ma? I've heard the name certainly, but I really don't know much about it."

"It's a dangerous bacterial infection that attacks the lungs, and is also called TB. What makes it even worse is that it can spread to other parts of the body as it has done to your father. One can get it just by breathing in the nasty germs from other people's coughing, sneezing – well just about anything where they open their mouth and you happen to be around them."

"How on earth did dad get it?"

"That's a good question because while it is contagious, it is not easy to catch. It comes from spending a lot of time around people who have it, so we suspect it was one of Jim's co-workers since, thank God, I don't have it. I'm also very careful when I go in to his room to wear a mask. Your father is very sick honey. He has lost a lot of weight, coughs up blood, and has a terrible pain in his chest. He does not want to eat, and I can no longer sleep with him as his night sweats keep him up. Besides, I do not want to get the disease especially since I am Jim's caregiver. I'll be honest in telling you that his doctor says he expects it will only be a matter of weeks before your daddy dies. By the time they diagnosed your father, who just thought he had a bad cough, any treatment they could have given him was already too late."

Tears came to Jack's eyes for all the time they did not have together. His mother patted him on the back while saying, "Thank you Jack for coming. I know it was not easy for you to do so owning a business and all. I just cannot find the words to express what your being here means to me, and I know when your father sees you, he will feel the same.

They then walked in to see the father. Jack could see traces of the father he once knew, but his initial view was one of shock. The full head of dark hair was gone and the father's appearance was very gaunt. However, there could be no denying the glint in the father's eyes when he saw Jack and mumbled the words, "My God, you are a grown man."

"Yes, I am Dad. That's what time does to you," Jack explained as he bent over to kiss his father on the cheek and then put on the face mask. Jack went on to feed his father some soup that his mother made, and they continued talking until the father fell asleep. Going to the room where he would sleep, Jack started to write his wife a letter. He mentally told himself he was going to write her every evening, and he would also enclose a page for Colleen.

The room was perfect for a young man. Jack thought what it might have been like to have moved here with his parents. The walls were painted a pale blue and the furniture was maple. The bedspread was plaid and masculine with colors of the light blue on the walls, navy blue and pale yellow. A desk was even provided. Jack sat down to write at the desk telling his wife about the trip there and how great it was to see his parents after all these years, despite his father's horrible illness. He also did explain more about what he had learned about his father's illness from his mother.

Jack estimated that he didn't expect to have his father around more than a couple of weeks, but as they all found out soon enough, the father had more stamina and the will to live than anyone ever expected.

7

On her way home for lunch one day, Colleen reached in the mailbox attached to the wall near the door on the front porch to get the mail that had been placed there by the mailman. In the 1940's, in this small town, mail delivery was twice a day in the morning and mid-afternoon. She flipped through the mail to see if her issue of Seventeen magazine had come. Instead, she saw that first letter from her father and after grabbing the mail, she opened the front door and ran through the house to show her mother.

The mother wanted to go to her room and read the letter in private, but she knew she should not do that at least for this very first letter. Once she realized Jack was going to enclose a page or two specifically for Colleen, Doris could feel free to read the letters she received in private in whatever room she chose. The two females salivated at each of the father's words and enjoyed his letters tremendously.

Both mother and daughter then sat down at the kitchen table to discuss their father's letter, the home in Missouri, the spry grandmother, the grandfather's condition as well as deciding what they should not say to the father in letters.

Since Jack left, and Colleen was in the bar more helping out by cleaning tables, and mopping the floor, the clientele took advantage of Jack's absence to make advances towards Colleen. For the most part she handled it well, retaliating with smart remarks back at the men. One day however, her uncle could not take it anymore and came from behind the bar grabbing one guy by the collar of his shirt and getting up in the guy's face saying, "If you ever touch my niece again and say those words you just said, it will be a sorry day in Hell for you, and you can count on my taking care of it." That evening the uncle talked with Doris and said he did not want Colleen helping in the bar anymore, and he told her why.

"What can we do without her? I am busy in the store, so I don't have time to clean up in the bar."

"I'll try and manage on my own until Jack gets back since you say it should only be a few weeks."

"OK, we'll see how it goes."

When a couple of weeks turned into many months, the brother eventually said he would ask the girl that Jack used before he left if she would come back. The brother could not understand why Jack let her go in the first place with the exception that he was probably concerned about money until he confirmed that the brother could come for sure.

During the summer months when a lot of male customers gathered outside the store and bar, some wise cracks towards Colleen continued. She always had a tart retort to give back in retaliation, and some thought the guys did this just to hear her response. Since no other adult was outside to hear the remarks made by the men, nothing was done to stop it with the exception that Doris did talk to the brother observing that with so many men hanging outside in clusters, a lot of women told her they did not want to come and pick up a few things at the store because the cat calls were embarrassing. They felt their knees would crumble as they walked past the men. These men were otherwise frequent good paying customers. Telling them not to hang outside during the summer months might be offensive and Doris was in a dilemma. For some odd reason, the men were more respectful when Jack ran things.

Back in Missouri, the father made a remarkable recovery once Jack arrived. Doctors were amazed at the stamina the older man acquired, though none of them said outright that the father was getting better. They were just shocked that the father appeared to be in some sort of remission.

Often, Jack and his mother enjoyed sitting outside on the back patio. One day the sky was a sort of greenish gray color and Jack remarked to his mother about it.

"That is the only thing I don't like about this area Jack, besides not having the ocean."

"What do you mean?"

"On occasion, we have some violent weather here – tornadoes, and they scare me to death. That is what that cement structure is in the far back, a storm shelter. However, sometimes the weather is so violent, we don't even want to go outside to get into it." At that point, the sirens went off.

"What the hell is that?"

"That's a tornado warning honey. Quick, we need to get inside and carry your father to the bathtub. One of us should stay in the tub with him, and the other can go to the other bathroom tub."

The storm came and went in the flash of a light. Fortunately, they received no damage, but the nearby town did. Jack thought that now he really wanted his mother to come and live with them.

Jack spent most of his days taking care of the father, reading to him, bathing him and helping him to eat. When the father napped, Jack would grocery shop for the mother or spend time in the yard with her chatting about life. Time was set aside daily to write home to his wife and daughter and he was thrilled almost every day to receive mail from them telling of the goings on back home. It was obvious that the mother and daughter were not telling him any negative stuff which was a little irritant because he felt he should always be the one to help with problems. Yet, he knew, they would always inform him if something serious were going on, and he pacified himself knowing this.

What was supposed to be a few weeks turned out to be almost a year. Towards the end, Jack spent a lot of the time preparing his mother for the worst. One day he had someone from the church baby sit the father while Jack took his mother to an attorney where her will was updated. Jack thought it wise to have his mother prepare her will in case something happened to her after the father died. Jack's objective was to have his mother come and live with his family on the east coast. Yet, he knew this was not going to be an easy decision. The mother had her own group of friends who stopped by often, and the people at her church were phenomenal with their help. The house was a small ranch house, so Jack was not worried about the upkeep of the home, and it would always be easy to get around should his mother become incapacitated. He already made arrangements for someone to cut the grass, and/or in the winter have someone take care of snow removal. Her neighbors were very friendly, and they all seemed to take care of one another, so that was also a plus. Should the mother not want to come immediately, Jack felt comfortable leaving her in Missouri for a while with the hope that seeing her granddaughter especially would help change her mind in the future.

Back home things were running as smoothly as possible, but the wife and daughter missed Jack miserably. The mother disliked not having her husband by her side when she went to bed, and Colleen always enjoyed joking with her dad. Without him around, things seemed rather routine and dull. No one would ever suspect that Colleen's sweet personality could ever be misinterpreted for something else and ultimately cause a horrible problem. However, that is exactly what happened.

8

Jack's father died a few weeks before spring began. His east coast family was looking forward to Jack's return. No one ever questioned if the wife and daughter were going to the funeral. The expense would be just too great. The day was lovely. Large cumulus clouds filled the azure colored sky, daffodils were sprouting hither and yon, and the forsythia bushes were in full bloom. Everything in the air smelled fresh and clean. Colleen stayed after school to help with the yearbook and took a minute to go to the girls' room. Margaret Chapman was washing her hands when Colleen walked into the area. There was no one else in sight considering the after-school hours. The two girls stood talking to one another when the unexpected happened.

Colleen had heard the word "queer" mentioned before and she knew the word meant something more than the usual "unconventional" connotation. The word itself did not sink in to Colleen, nor did she realize it had another meaning. The suggested meaning during the 1940's otherwise really did not register with her. Margaret, in today's world, would have been called a lesbian or gay, but the words meant nothing to Colleen. Nor, did most people call Margaret queer. When Margaret could see that no one else was in the area, especially since they were by the sinks which had a wall in between the sinks and the toilets, she gently pulled Colleen towards her. She had misinterpreted Colleen's friendliness. Colleen at first thought she was bringing her close because she saw something on her dress she was going to remove. Déjà vu hit Colleen when instead, Margie grabbed Colleen and tried to kiss her.

Colleen backed away while saying, "Margaret, what the heck are you doing?" She attempted to push Margaret away, but the poor child was thinking Colleen wanted her same desires and persisted.

Just as Colleen showed some annoyance while pushing Margaret away, a group of other girls on the junior varsity cheerleading squad all came in and saw what they interpreted as anger from Colleen. In fact, one girl yelled out "cool down Colleen."

Colleen immediately left the area, her face flushed and full of an astonished look. She never got to use the facilities which had been her original intended purpose. People saw her fast-paced walking through the halls and whispered to themselves and each other that this did not look like the usual Colleen. They wondered what caused her to look the way she did. When she entered the yearbook room everyone looked up and quickly questioned Colleen as to if something happened to her to cause her unusual appearance. Upon hearing their questioning, tears started to roll down Colleen's cheeks even though she tried to maintain some type of composure. "I'll be alright," she said. "I'm just not feeling well, and I think I'll go on home." One of the guys offered to walk her home and Colleen did not say no. She was afraid of perhaps seeing Margaret again. Once home, her mother became worried and told Colleen to go to her room and lie down. Mrs. O'Conner said she would come up to take care of her as soon as she got someone to help in the store. Since her Dad was due home the next day, Doris even let her daughter stay home from school that day as well. She was convinced that the excitement of her father returning had caused her daughter to become unsettled which could not have been further from the truth. Yet, Colleen somehow felt she had done something wrong. Fearful that she would get in trouble, Colleen would not tell anyone what had happened.

Despite what Colleen had experienced, the thrill of seeing her father that day temporarily eased her scary thoughts. The morning was sunny and bright, just the type of day one would want to celebrate a happy occasion. Doris was busy in the kitchen when Colleen walked in with her baby doll pajamas and curly hair out of control and framing her beautiful face. "Whatcha doing Ma?"

"I'm fixing your father a feast of Kings with all his favorite foods."

"It smells delicious in here. What time do you expect Dad to arrive?"

"Some time around 1:30 this afternoon.

"Ok. After breakfast, I'll go upstairs and get ready, and I'll finish off in the kitchen so you can make yourself beautiful for dad."

Doris gave her daughter a huge hug, a big smile and a kiss on the cheek. "Are you feeling better today sweetheart?"

The mother's words reminded Colleen of what had occurred the day before, but she immediately tried to reassure her mother she was feeling fine.

The homecoming could not have been better. Mother and daughter were ecstatic to have Jack home, and he could not have been more thrilled to be there. Relaxing all day, Jack told them everything about being with his parents once again. There was talk about having the mother come and live with them, but Jack had told them she would be hard to convince. The house was lovely and her neighbors were great, so for the time being Jack was not concerned. "We'll take baby steps honey. If we let her think she is making this decision on her own, maybe some day we can convince her to come back east. It also may mean exhuming dad's body so they can both be buried together, but that's a future conversation. With that he grabbed both his wife and daughter for the millionth time to give them another huge hug and kiss. "God, how I missed the two of you. Now, let's talk about life back here in this sweet town."

The first day everyone left the family alone to reunite. The second day, a Saturday, several stopped by bringing gifts of food or delicacies. Jack whispered to his wife, "You might think one of us died," when the umpteenth platter was brought and placed on the kitchen counter. Of course, they all stayed for some conversation and something to drink.

It was late that afternoon when a police vehicle parked in front of the business. Two police officers got out of the car. Colleen was up in her room and did not see the officers. She kept replaying the scene in the girls' room over and over in her head trying to think of what she did wrong. She was also really scared of returning to school on Monday.

At first Jack thought the police were going to the bar and really was not concerned when he saw their vehicle. However, instead of walking to the bar door, they came up on the porch and knocked on the O'Conner's front door. Jack greeted the two officers by their name, since just about everyone knew everyone else in the small town.

Doris came in the room when she heard the knock on the front door. Upon seeing the two men in uniform, Doris offered them a seat and something to eat and drink. "Sorry, Doris, we are not here for a social call. We are here to see Colleen, if she is home."

Both Jack and Doris were taken aback by the officers' request.

"Colleen is home, but maybe we can help you," said John.

"This issue involves only your daughter, but you are certainly allowed to stay in the room while we question her."

Both parents stood there staring at the officers, their minds thinking all types of questions, but neither of them could come up with any answers. Why on earth would the police want to talk to their beautiful daughter?

"Mam?" said one officer, hoping to jar at least one of the parents out of the trance they appeared to be having. "Is it possible we could speak to your daughter?"

Doris immediately adjusted her posture while apologizing to the police. "I'll be right down," Doris said as she walked up the stairs to get Colleen.

Colleen was spread out on her bed with school books and papers thrown all over the entire bedspread. Doris's first inclination was to ask Colleen if it would not be easier to do her homework at her desk until she remembered why she came upstairs in the first place. "Honey, can you please come downstairs?"

"Sure, Mom, I'll be down in about fifteen minutes. By the way, I heard some voices downstairs. Is it our neighbors?"

"No, it is the police, and they only want to talk to you."

Colleen immediately sat up and inquired why.

"I don't know honey, but you need to come down now."

Getting up off the bed, fear overwhelmed Colleen. Never before had the police wanted to question her about anything. Instead of acting composed, Colleen was rattled and somewhat frightened, but she followed her mother downstairs.

The officers, whom Jack had offered a seat, immediately stood when the two women entered the room.

While offering handshakes to Colleen, the older officer said to her, "We just have a few questions to ask you Colleen. We do not intend to be long."

"Yes sir," was all Colleen could manage to get out of her mouth. "Do you know Margaret Chapman?"

"Yes, I know Margie."

Doris interrupted by saying that Colleen and her friends were some of the first girls to befriend Margaret when they moved to town. Margaret's mother even told me how impressed she was by the girls' kindness.

"I'm sure Mam, but could you please let Colleen answer the questions."

"Why?" Colleen asked the officer.

"We understand you and Margaret had a little confrontation in the girls' room."

Thinking of what happened, and not wanting to get Margaret in trouble, or to let out her secret, Colleen became extremely scared and could not speak.

"Did you see Margaret in the girls' rest room?"

Colleen just shook her head to indicate yes.

"Were you having a fight?"

"Who told you this," asked Colleen, while wondering if Margaret was telling this to the police.

"Apparently, the girls' J V cheerleading team came in to the room when the two of you were fighting."

Again, Colleen clammed shut.

"What difference does it make sir? Girls get in arguments all the time. That is no reason to question our daughter," inquired Jack.

"Mr. O'Conner. Margaret's body was found murdered in the wooded area behind the female rest room, and your daughter was seen having an argument with the deceased."

At this, all three members of the family looked up in shock.

Jack broke the silence by saying, "That's enough questioning now sir. This news is a shock to all of us. We would like time to digest what we just heard."

Sensing that they were not going to get much more out of Colleen, the two officers quietly said, "We are sorry to have bothered you and your family Mr. O'Conner, we'll let ourselves out the door."

The family all remained in a stupor. First of all, murder just did not happen in this small town. Secondly, to have the murder be someone the family knew was even more of a shock. They remained lethargic for several minutes until Doris finally said, "What are we going to do?"

9

Within hours, news about the murder had spread all over town. Most were in disbelief not only about the murder, but that the police actually thought Colleen had committed such a horrible act. While the majority in the town were skeptical that Colleen had anything to do with the murder and were convinced the police had the story wrong, those that were jealous of Colleen convinced themselves she was indeed the murderer. They knew all along Colleen had this violent streak in her. They just could not wait to smear this lovely child.

In the Wagner household, a conversation was going on of a different nature. Mia was disheartened and disbelieving. She knew one of her best friends was not capable of murdering another friend, so she was incredulous of what she heard about Colleen. The fact that Margie was murdered was quite another story. She and her Mom had gone out to see Mrs. Chapman with a casserole and to convey their sorrow. The food though was left with someone taking over in the house. She told Mia and her mother that Mrs. Chapman had to be sedated and was in a terrible state of mind. She also asked if they would be kind enough to tell as many people as they could that now was not a good time to pay their respects and they can blame me. "I'm Eleanor, and I am Mrs. Chapman's sister from the city. The funeral will also be private." They did not feel anyone in the family was up to a spectacle that could occur when a high school student is murdered.

Back home again, Mr. Wagner was saying to Mia's mom, "That phone call was Mr. O'Conner. He wants me to take Colleen's case. He said he did not care that I usually did not defend accused murderers. He knew such a thing was not common in our area. But, he said, Colleen felt comfortable around me and he thought I would be the best lawyer for his daughter."

Mia was listening to the conversation from another room. Mrs. Wagner said, "I don't think you should hon. We are too close to the situation. And, we are also prejudiced in knowing Colleen could not do such a thing."

"It is hard for me to tell Jack no though."

When Mia heard that, she felt she had to butt in. "Dad, please take the case. I know you will be great, and Colleen likes you. You have to defend her. Please Dad?"

"I don't think I can sweetheart. Colleen is in a sense like another daughter to me. You two are so close, I don't know if I can be fair in my thinking."

Mrs. Wagner popped up then and said, "If anyone is fair, it is you. You might not take this case, but I won't let you not take it on those grounds."

"Please say yes Dad, please?"

"Give me some time to digest this whole scenario. I promise you Mia, I'll have an answer tomorrow."

Over on Main Boulevard, the conversation had another tone, but in many ways, it was just as grim and sad. All the Gelmans just could not comprehend any of what they had heard.

Mrs. Gelman was telling Dr. Gelman that she just knew all his patients would want to talk about what happened because they knew the girls were so close.

"Well, dear, that's not going to be a problem for me as I really don't know what happened. It will be easy to tell the truth. Besides, being a physician, I have a way of stopping conversations in their track without offending anyone by suggesting the patient and I have more important things to discuss concerning them. That shuts them up every time."

"You don't know anything besides the rumors, do you honey?" The question was meant for Barbara.

"No Mom, I honestly don't. The day of the supposed confrontation Colleen stayed to do yearbook stuff, so Mia and I walked home together without her."

Mrs. Gelman just stood there shaking her head in wonderment. "My heart so goes out to all the O'Conners."

Dr. Gelman piped in that he could not even begin to imagine what they were experiencing.

* * *

Barbara called Mia and invited her over for the afternoon. She explained to Mia that she was also going to call Colleen in the hope they could maintain some sort of normalcy in a situation that was nothing like normal.

"That's a great idea Barb. I'll be over in about an hour, and good luck convincing Colleen she should come as well."

When Barbara called Colleen's home, the mother answered the phone. Barbara decided to ask the mother before asking Colleen in the hope that she would assert her influence to convince Colleen to go to Barbara's house.

"Hi, Mrs. O'Conner. Do you think Colleen is up to coming over to my house for the afternoon? I thought the break might do her good. Mia will also be here."

"I'm not exactly sure how Colleen feels about going out, and I am concerned when the weekend is over if she is even going to want to go to school. I do think spending time with the two of you would be great for her. Hold on honey while I get her."

Mrs. O'Conner walked up to her daughter's room, and knocked gently. When she heard Colleen say to come in, Mrs. O'Conner opened the door and told Colleen she was wanted on the phone.

Fear showed in Colleen's face as she inquired of her mother who would want to talk to her.

"It's Barbara. She's asking you and Mia to go to her house this afternoon for a few hours."

Colleen immediately began shaking her head. "No, Mom, I don't want to go."

"Look Colleen, I will sort of insist you go. If you stay home all the time people will get the impression that maybe you are guilty. You have got to show them that you are not."

"I really don't feel like going, but I think I understand your point of view."

"I'll even drive you over there this time and pick you up, if you think that will make it easier for you. Either way, Barbara is on the phone asking for you. So, please pick up the phone and talk to her."

The mother could hear Colleen say hello and attempted to listen to the conversation though this was not something she usually did. After about fifteen minutes, it did sound like Colleen agreed to go. The mother ran to the couch to make it appear she had been sitting there all along.

"Does that offer still stand to drive me over to the Gelman's?"

"Of course, dear. You can call me any time you are ready to come home."

The two got in the family car and drove the short distance to Main Boulevard and the Gelman's home. Mia and Barbara were already standing behind the screen door excited to see their friend. They both ran outside to get her and to say hello to Mrs. O'Conner.

The two friends attempted to act normal, but there was nothing normal about the whole situation. Inevitably, talk got around to what had occurred. The dilemma for Colleen still existed, however. She had some type of loyalty to Margie and did not want to tell her friends the reason she had the confrontation in the first place. Barbara and Mia were kind enough not to push the matter. Finally, Colleen did say, "I hope you understand that whatever caused the two of us to be irritated would never cause me to be so volatile that I would ever murder Margie, or anyone else for that matter."

"We know that, Colleen. The subject is dropped."

The girls decided to make some cookies, and then they went up to Barbara's Room to glance through Seventeen magazine. They also experimented with some of Mrs. Gelman's old makeup she had given to Barbara which she originally intended to throw away. Barbara asked if she could have it to use it for fun.

Eventually, the talk did get around to school, and Colleen admitted she was fearful of returning. The girls assured her they would fend off any untoward remarks. They promised to stick by her side and ward off any hecklers. Colleen had not been officially charged with anything yet, so she was free to roam around like normal. If she could get through the next few weeks at school and graduation, summer break would soon be upon them. Colleen did decide to no longer work on the yearbook, however. It was practically finished anyway and would be printed soon. Going there, she had decided, might trigger bad memories she would rather forget.

10

Monday rolled around way too soon. Colleen enjoyed spending Sunday afternoon with her two best friends. It was just the break she needed, but here it was Monday already, and she was terrified about going to school. This was probably the first time in her life where she feared going to school. The smile that usually brightened her face was now more a look of concern.

Her two friends awakened early as they wanted to be sure to go directly to Colleen's house to pick her up. This had not been their usual routine, but this is what they planned to do until school ended that summer. They waited outside Colleen's house sitting on the front steps. Colleen's mother saw them there and opened the door to invite them inside. The girls chose to sit outside. It was a nice day weather-wise, and they explained they did not want to upset Colleen's daily routine by having to make unexpected conversation. The mother said a secret prayer under her breath for these two sweet supporters of her daughter. She could not help but be worried about her daughter going to school this day.

Those friends they met along the way that were also walking to school were not the type to be judgmental, and they all liked Colleen, so that was a plus. When they passed on the street, they offered the group a friendly greeting and nothing was said about what had occurred. Passing groups of people in front of the school was quite another story. A group of girls who were transported by bus from a nearby community shouted out "Murderer." Colleen was so tempted to turn around and run home, but each of her two friends wrapped their arms around Colleen's arms from both sides. They whispered for Colleen to be quiet and they forced her to just keep walking. Once inside the hallway, another group that included some guys who felt Colleen would never pay them any attention with her good looks, also yelled out "Murderer!" The girls kept walking.

Classroom time was a little more tolerable. Having her friends in all her classes really helped. All day, however, Colleen had the urge to use the girls' room, but refused to go anywhere near it. This was going to be a problem if she attended school until they graduated. Her two friends talked about this in private. They came up with a plan to have the girls both take her between second and third period since their next class was right across the hall from the prior class, and they would have more time. The first day they planned this, which was Colleen's second day back, they could hardly convince her to go with them. The urge was there, but Colleen felt it would have been better not going at all. However, she finally acquiesced.

Graduation turned out to be more fun than anticipated. Things went along smoothly until the day after graduation when the police came to the O'Conner's home and told the parents their daughter was under arrest. Doris nearly fainted had it not been for her husband catching her. Colleen heard her mother scream and ran downstairs only to see her mother and father standing there with the same two policemen who had come to her house before.

"What's wrong?" The words were barely out of Colleen's mouth when the mother almost fainted again.

The father put his arms around his daughter and explained that she was being arrested for the murder of Margaret.

Colleen immediately sat on the couch in disbelief.

"I'm afraid she has to come with us Sir," said the policeman who had done most of the talking the first time.

"You are kidding of course."

"No sir. I am very serious."

"Why must you take her? She is not a threat to society."

"Where are you taking her?" Doris had inquired after looking up in disbelief.

"To the detention facility on Morris Road."

Doris grabbed her daughter while saying, "No, no, you cannot take her there. Absolutely not!"

"I'm sorry mam, but she will be going. We don't know if she is a threat, or not."

"Oh, dear God. Help me. My daughter cannot go there."

The officer just did not know how to handle the situation. The daughter looked no more like a criminal than his own child, yet those were his orders – to take the child.

All he could say was, "I'm sorry mam."

The five of them stood for a long time in silence until the mother finally said, "Can I go with her?"

The other cop said, "No, mam, you may not."

Doris looked up with such a pleading look on her face that the first cop did say, "If you like, Mrs. O'Conner, you can ride with us and stay there until we get your daughter settled, but then you will have to leave."

"If I sat where you first enter in a sort of lobby area, there is nothing to say I can't stay there, right?"

In frustration, the policeman just shook his head while explaining to Colleen, who wanted to go upstairs to get some things, that all she needed were the clothes on her back.

The father said, "I'll follow you, and hopefully my wife can ride in the backseat of your car with my daughter."

Not wanting to cause any more unnecessary problems, the law officers agreed.

As soon as Mrs. O'Conner saw the jail (as essentially, that is what it looked like), she became fidgety and almost out of control. When someone came to take her daughter, Mrs. O'Conner grabbed her daughter's dress and would not release the child. All the while, tears were streaming down both the mother's and daughter's faces.

During the wee hours of the morning, Jack tried to convince his wife to leave the facility, but she would have none of his pleading. "Well, honey, I have to go. The store will be opening in an hour and I need to get things ready."

"Go, go!" Doris was sharp in her response which did not follow her usual disposition.

Momentarily, Jack was concerned if he should leave his wife, but secretly he felt better knowing she was close by his daughter. Driving home, Jack felt extremely sullen. He decided he would call Mr. Wagner as soon as the office opened; Mia's Dad had already agreed to take the case if needed.

11

Sleep did not come to Colleen her first night in jail. People's voices, who were supposed to be asleep, kept echoing off the walls. She was also put in a room with another older hardened woman who made Colleen feel very uncomfortable. All rules of privacy went out the door. Colleen nearly had to force herself to go to the bathroom as bad as the urge to go threatened her. She hated to even think of having a bowel movement there. The food was just ok though she only was given a late dinner, if that is what you want to call it. Some of it seemed like slop to her for want of a better name.

Exhaustion filled her body just from the sheer thought of being in a prison. Despite placing her head on the cot pillow as she attempted to rest, her brain was wide awake with thoughts. She hated the communal showers when morning finally arrived. Yet, she did feel if she showered it might wipe away some of the drudge of being in jail. Her encounter with Margie made her trust no one, and the comments from the other women jailers did not help as they echoed, "Hey Beauty, want to get together later, or now even?" For some unknown reason the hardened roommate wanted to take Colleen under her wing. When she indicated to Colleen to stick by her and she would handle the "smart asses", as she called them, Colleen decided to do just as she said.

Reformatories for just women were established in many states in the 1940's because of the history of male abuse of females that were incarcerated. Often, females were impregnated by male guards, so these reformatories were established. Their location was however usually far out in the country atmosphere, and the parents of Colleen hoped she would not have to be sent so far away.

Mr. Wagner met with the parents saying he was having a hard time getting Colleen released on bail because of the nature of her crime.

"She's not a murderer," said Mrs. O'Connor.

"I know that, but being accused of murder is a serious offense, and I do not have it within my power to override that fact."

"Dear God, what can we do?" Jack was beside himself.

The attorney said, "I went to the jail and briefly talked to Colleen this morning. She told me that her cell mate sort of took Colleen under her wing. The cell mate demands a certain decorum of response from the other inmates who for some odd reason either fear or respect her, and that in turn benefits Colleen. For a few weeks, I will at least request Colleen stay where she is. Of course, I don't know how long that cell mate will be incarcerated, or if she will be moved to another facility. For the time being, the situation as it now looks appears to be working in Colleen's favor and therefore, so far, so good."

Doris sighed in resignation. She just could not imagine things getting worse than they already were. All she wanted was to have her lovely Colleen home again.

What Mr. Wagner did not say was that he had the feeling Colleen was withholding something. He tried hard to figure out what it was, but he could not get Colleen to reveal it.

It was later in the afternoon after the prisoners had spent time in the fresh air, and after Colleen had returned to her cell that footsteps could be heard coming down the hallway with periodic sounds of keys being used and metal doors slamming. The footsteps got close to Colleen's cell and stopped. She looked up to see Mr. Wagner along with a guard, and she did not quite understand at first why he came to see her again.

The cellmate was taken temporarily to another area for some unknown reason, so Mr. Wagner and Colleen were left along together in her cell. Mr. Wagner explained at that time that this visit was more formal because he had been chosen by her parents to represent Colleen, and he had a few questions to ask her.

Colleen did not say anything, but she did shake her head as though to say she understood.

"Can you tell me about the confrontation you had with Margie in the girls' room."

"There is nothing to tell really. We had a little disagreement is all."

"It is my understanding from the girls on the cheerleading squad that they saw you push Margie away in anger."

"Well, sir, what they saw, and what actually happened is subject to interpretation."

"True, but just what were the two of you arguing about?"

Colleen sat for a long time and did not respond. Her mind was moving in circles. I can't spread the rumor that Margie was gay. They will think that I am making this up, and anyway, I could not reveal that about my friend. Her loyalty was without reason.

"Colleen? Did you hear my question?"

"I don't remember." Now, she really felt bad because she purposely told a lie to someone she respected.

Sensing that he was not going to get more information from Colleen, he stood to go. As he was preparing to leave, Mr. Wagner said to Colleen, "I have a feeling, for some odd reason, that you are not being honest with me. I cannot defend you properly if I am not privy to all the pertinent information as you know it."

"Yes, sir."

"I will be available if you feel you need me any time of the day or night. Here is my card with a phone number where I can be reached. Even if you should lose the card, tell one of the guards to contact me as they have our numbers on record. Oh, by the way, the arraignment is set for Tuesday of next week."

"What's an arraignment?"

"That is where you will be officially charged. So far, they continue to feel that a "No Bond" will still apply in your case as an alleged murderer, but we'll see what the judge says on Tuesday. You will also get to plead guilty, or not guilty that day. The court date for your trial will be given at that time."

"Naturally I'll plead not guilty. Did you doubt that sir?"

"No, Colleen. That is just the proper procedure and your two choices. I had no doubt you will plead not guilty."

Mr. Wagner assured Colleen that the court date would be sooner rather than later, and he said that if she did not get released to her parents, he was going to attempt to get her to stay at the local facility. When Mr. Wagner did leave, Colleen was sad to see a familiar face go. She walked around the cell and sat down once again. As she did so, she examined the walls and the barren color of the cell. She hated what they called the "potty" that they were forced to use. The open bars on one side of the cell was a constant reminder that you would not have any privacy while confined there. She mentally prayed she would not be sent to solitary confinement about which she knew nothing except for what she had seen in movies. She did not even know if solitary confinement was a consideration for her. Momentarily, Colleen became claustrophobic. When this happened, she immediately started to do jumping jacks to distract herself when her cell mate returned. She was almost happy to see her, but back in her cell the mate acquired her evil attitude once again that was missing when she took Colleen under her control during the time the other inmates were around.

Not knowing what else to do at this point, Colleen quietly sat down to pray in the least obvious manner possible. She prayed that Margie's real killer would be found. She also prayed she could withstand any obstacles thrown her way while in jail.

Colleen's parents suffered unimaginably. It was almost too much to work in the store or bar. For some reason, people felt at those locations, they could ask anything their hearts desired. Yet, the parents really did not want to discuss their private matters with anyone else. This caused friction in the marriage that normally would not be there.

The only blessing out of all of this was when Jack's mother in Missouri heard of the horror of her granddaughter being incarcerated and charged with murder. She decided the only proper thing to do was to come east and help out in any way that was deemed necessary. Even if she was only needed as a sounding board, her presence, she felt, was needed.

Jack was thrilled she was coming, but Doris was not so sure. She did not really know her mother-in-law. Having another person to be concerned about figured out in Doris's mind to be more of a chore than a help. All she wanted to do right now was wallow in her own sadness. However,

Mrs. O'Conner was family after all, and Doris was brought up with the proper respect to acknowledge that fact. Doris fixed up a spare room to make it homier in atmosphere. Doing this did provide an element of appreciated distraction. The next day Jack was going to pick his mother up at the train station and Doris got someone to tend the store so that she could ride along with him. She was anxious to meet this woman who had raised a son to be such a fine young man. This was the mother of her husband that she loved dearly.

The elder Mrs. O'Conner stepped off the train looking more elegant than Doris ever imagined. The hat that looked so stylish on her head, matched the wool material and maroon color of the coat on her back. Her samsonite suitcase was of the size where it looked like Mrs. O'Conner was going to stay as long as needed. She wore black gloves and black pump shoes that had a slight heel. Her gray hair appeared to be elegantly coiffed under the hat. This short, slim woman exuded confidence that gave all around her a reassuring feeling.

Once spotting Jack, the smile on Mrs. O'Conner's face was endearing. The first thing she did when meeting Doris was to wrap her in a warm embrace. As far as Doris was concerned, this is just what the doctor ordered. Hmm, maybe it won't be so bad having my mother-in-law here after all, thought Doris.

12

Thinking he should explain what was to happen at the arraignment, Mr. Wagner dropped by the O'Conner home. The elder Mrs. O'Conner said she would get her son from the bar area. When they both returned, Jack asked if Mr. Wagner had met his mother. "I figured that was your mother, as I heard from the gossip mill that she was visiting from Missouri."

After a more formal introduction, and after Doris brought in some lemonade and cookies as a snack, Mr. Wagner told the parents what to expect at Tuesday's arraignment.

Jack's mother spoke asking if it would be ok if she accompanied her son and his wife to the courthouse."

"Of course. I did hear that Mrs. Chapman, Margie's mother, has hired a high-profile attorney from New York City. Unfortunately, this small town is going to be swarming with journalists from all the major newspapers. I do fear a bit of a fiasco competing with someone of that stature."

"If there is one thing I am sure about Tom, is that you are the best attorney our daughter could have, so no worry there. Besides, often these highfalutin lawyers come across as pompous and pretentious in a small-town atmosphere. I remember seeing them once at another area. They come in with their fancy limos, expensive clothing and an entourage that would indicate a famous person was being tried – they just looked out of place, and it prejudices the people from around here," said Jack.

"Should that be the case, we are going to have a big fight on our hands before the trial even starts. They will want to change the venue to another town and seek jurors who could care less of the outcome."

"God, I hope you don't let that happen."

"I can only try my best. Sometimes, money counts, and these people have loads of it. However, we'll cross that bridge when we come to it. I'll leave now unless you have more questions about Tuesday."

"No Tom. We'll see you on Tuesday."

Tom shook Jack's mother's hand while saying it was a pleasure meeting her.

At dinner that evening, Cora said she thought they had a good attorney. Attempting to reassure her family she further said, "I'm confident everything is going to turn out fine."

Doris and Jack only wished they could be as confident as Jack's mother.

* * *

Barbara and Mia visited their friend at the jail and were completely out of their element. While Colleen was thrilled to see them, of course, it made her quite uncomfortable to have her friends see her in that surrounding. The two girls felt the same way as they looked around. They did not look like the typical jail visitor.

On the way home, they stopped at the soda shop to discuss what they experienced. They picked a booth in the back area hoping none of their school friends would see them. Most likely, the majority were either at their place of employment, or they were swimming in one of the lakes because it was a warm, sticky summer day. In fact, the girls thought about going swimming themselves, but the interior of the soda shop was dark and with the overhead fans blowing, they felt cool there so decided they would skip swimming that day. Both girls were helping at their father's places of work. Barbara assisted at the front desk of her father's office while the normal receptionist took her vacation and to give her mother a summer break. The attorney's office was thrilled to have Mia take care of filing the paperwork that was getting out of hand. The girls were excited to get their meager pay checks each week, and in Mia's case she could walk to work. Barbara, of course, did not even have to leave her home.

Of course, all they could talk about was their friend Colleen. The summer months just were not the same without having their friend share in the excitement. Plus, they both were so afraid of what might happen to Colleen.

Barbara said, "She looks good considering, and Colleen mentioned that her cell mate enjoyed doing Colleen's hair."

"It must be terrible though taking communal showers. Reminds me of showering after gym." mentioned Mia.

"I hate doing that in gym, and I can't even imagine doing so in jail. Also, let's face it, the meals can't compare to what our mothers make for us daily."

"I did notice that Colleen looked slimmer. Maybe it was the jail clothes, but she did look thinner."

Mentioning her concern, Barbara supposed that if Colleen lost any more weight, she would be way too skinny.

"Hmm," said Mia, "I wonder if we are allowed to bring her food. You are correct in that right now she looks great considering. However, she would look emaciated if she were to lose more weight."

"I don't know. I just remember those movies where people used to sneak objects in cakes that might help the prisoner escape. Thinking that, I would probably imagine they do not want us bringing anything to our friend. Though, it would not hurt to ask, I suppose."

"Do you get the feeling that Colleen is withholding information from us?"

"Yea, I got that same sensation, but what it might be is a concern."

Mia and Barbara had each ordered a Sundae and a coke which the waitress brought to them at that time. Also, at the same time, a bunch of students they knew came into the store and immediately saw the girls and drifted to the back to talk to them. So much for privacy whispered each girl to the other.

Once home, the girls were bombarded with questions about their visit by their parents. Willing to get their feelings off their chest, the girls were eager to express their views.

Mia mentioned to her mom and dad that she had the feeling Colleen tried to withhold information. Her mother inquired why she would do such a thing. The father on the other hand said, "You know, Mia, I get the same feeling every time I talk to her. I am now really concerned knowing she won't even tell you. Gosh, if she won't tell her two best friends in the world, I have no hope she will tell me. What on earth do you think is bothering her so much that she can't tell any of us?"

"I don't know Dad, but I have the feeling she thinks whatever it is could be bad."

"How can I try a case if Colleen is hiding valuable information?"

"It's indeed a puzzle," piped in Mrs. Wagner.

13

Not only was Colleen losing weight, but Mrs. O'Conner, despite her good cooking, could not help but notice both Doris and Jack were losing weight as well. She knew their concerns about their daughter, so instead of bringing their lost weight to their attention, she just kept preparing healthy meals in the hope they might get their appetites back.

In the big city, Mr. & Mrs. Chapman were having one of the biggest arguments ever while in their ultra-modern and sleek penthouse apartment. Mr. Chapman was furious because he never wanted to move to the small town in the first place.

"I told you we should not move there. Margie's gender preferences were not going to change after we moved there. Your presumptions were ridiculous and ignorant."

"Why do you say that? You are not a physician. What do you know?"

"I know if you are gay you cannot change the way you feel."

"You're just saying that because you did not want to move out of the city in the first place."

"My God, will you ever understand that the reason we moved away was just stupid." Their voices were getting louder and louder. "How senseless to think that if we moved to a small town you could get Margie to change her feelings. At least in the city people are more tolerant. That was right up there with your ridiculous idea of first sending her to conversion therapy. Margie had friends like her here in the city. She was very happy, and you ruined it all."

"There you go, blaming me. Always, when something doesn't go your way, you blame me."

"Just shut up. I've had enough. Yes, I blame you for being the cause of our daughter's murder."

Mrs. Chapman got right up in her husband's face and screamed even louder. "I DID NOT MURDER MY DAUGHTER. How can you even suggest such a thing?"

"Well, if we had not moved, Margie would still be alive."

"You don't know that, so get that damn idea out of your head."

"What is your solution? If that Colleen girl tells everyone our daughter was gay, the very knowledge you were trying to avoid will be plastered all over the newspapers both here in the city, and certainly it will be big news in that small town."

"Why do you think Margie told Colleen? Maybe she doesn't even know."

"That's the problem. We DON'T know. The only way we could find out for sure is ask her, and if she doesn't know, we'll have let the cat out of the bag."

"I can't go back there. Ever! Tell Eleanor to put the house up for sale. I'll never return to that area again. They are mean, nasty people."

"Oh, come on now. Don't blame everyone in that town for one depraved jerk. We stand to lose a lot of money if we sell now."

"I DON'T CARE," she screamed. "What good is the money without our precious Margie. WHAT GOOD IS IT? ANSWER ME."

At that outburst, Mr. Chapman grabbed his brief case and stormed out of the apartment, slamming the door behind him.

"Right, run away. That's going to solve everything!" Mrs. Chapman was beside herself. Who could she yell at now since her husband left? She picked up the phone and dialed her sister.

"Hello?" It felt good to hear her sister's sweet voice. How fortunate the family was wealthy, and her sister Eleanor could just go and stay in the house for a while since she had no job to concern her. But her sister did not sound like her old self. "What's wrong babe?"

"The home in this small town is lovely, but it is so far out in the sticks, and I started to think to myself, what if Colleen isn't the murderer? Might the killer come to the house looking for me? I'm really not sure I want to stay here anymore."

"I just told Paul I want to sell the house. I never want to go back there. We've been arguing ever since we returned. Paul thinks Margie would still be alive if we had not moved, and I can't give you an answer about the house because he just left and was very angry. I tell you what. Get in touch with a realtor, if only to have someone looking out for the house, and tomorrow you pack up and have the limo driver take you back here. Neither one of us has been going into the office. Though, we do have good assistants running the place when we are not there. They also call us for our advice on important matters. I told them it will be months since I expect to return."

"I think I will do as you say. They really think that Colleen did it, but somehow to me, it just doesn't make sense. Maybe you can rent the house with the intention of selling it in the future, but at least I'll tell the realtor you are considering many options. I've got a pencil handy, so give me the name of the realtor you want me to call."

* * *

It was two whole days before Paul returned to the penthouse. Unbeknown to his wife, he slept in the cot at the office at night and just roamed the streets during the day. On occasion, he would venture into a shop to look around or to get a bite to eat. The walking in the city was like an endorphin to him helping to keep his mind distracted and free from the pain concerning the loss of his daughter. At this moment, as much as he loved his wife, the idea of getting a divorce did cross his mind. Yes, part of it was because he blamed her for the murder of his daughter – but another part of him knew he was being irrational. If he were being honest, he would have to acknowledge that he secretly always wanted to try living in a small-town atmosphere, but now it was easy to just blame his wife.

He was unaware that his sister-in-law had returned the day before. Emily had begged her sister to stay with them, but Eleanor felt it better to be at her own place when Paul returned. She knew both her sister and brother-in-law had a lot to discuss and hopefully, by now, they had worked out their anger.

Emily was telling her sister after she arrived that the only way she would be going to the courtroom is if they changed the venue to another area. "I just can't step another foot in that town."

"That's so unfortunate," said Eleanor. "I found the people there to be so nice and friendly. It's just that your house was too far out in the woods. However, I must admit I enjoyed having the pool all to myself. The only one ever around constantly was the limo driver who had his own small, but lovely place on the grounds. So, it wasn't that I was completely alone, but the house just felt lonely. Of course, a lot of that I'm sure had to do with losing Margie."

"I never felt too comfortable in that town. I don't know what it was."

"Well, you don't dress like the women there do. You do expose a little more of your body, and you and Paul are much more demonstrative in person than those people in that small town. I suppose that had a lot to do with it."

"Was I supposed to change my style just because we moved there?"

"You surely heard the expression, something like, when in Rome, do as the Romans do?"

"Are you saying my clothes and my actions caused Margie to be murdered?"

"Don't change the subject, Emily. You're the one who said you never felt comfortable while living there, and I just gave you some reasons why perhaps you felt that way. Maybe the people did not even mind. Perhaps they secretly wished they could act like you. However, you must have instinctively known you were acting differently from the rest of them, and it is you yourself that made you uncomfortable, not the people there."

"Why do you always have to make so much damn sense. Either way, I didn't feel comfortable there, and I'm happy to never go back. Oh God, Eleanor, I miss my daughter so much. We were always so close, and now she is gone – forever!"

"I know honey." Eleanor walked up to her sister and wrapped her arms around her. Both women had a good cry into each other's shoulders.

Emily finally broke loose to grab a tissue and said, "I can't believe Colleen murdered Margie either. Those three lovely girls were so kind to Margie when we moved there that it just doesn't make sense. However, what in the heck could they have been arguing about anyway?"

"You don't think Margie approached Colleen sexually, do you? And, that is what made her angry?" Emily had explained why they were moving in the first place, so Eleanor was privy to all the information concerning Margie. She thought her sister really dumb on the subject, but it was none of her business, so she did not interfere.

"I just don't know."

14

Tuesday morning rolled around soon enough. This was the day of the arraignment. Colleen did not have to go if she did not want to, but she thought that anything that would take her away from the jail would be better than staying in it. Besides, Mr. Wagner said she would be taken in the back way in case there were any spectators making a scene. She also knew her relatives and friends would be there – they hoped to give her moral support in front of the judge.

In the minutes before the proceedings, Colleen's parents were discussing the process with Mr. Wagner. Mrs. O'Conner was complaining that while in jail her daughter had been frisked and fingerprinted. "They are already treating her like she committed the murder," she complained.

"Yes, this world war we are now experiencing has seen a boom in the collection of fingerprinting by the Federal Bureau of Investigation, or FBI, due to wartime vigilance. Soldiers, foreign agents, draft dodgers, potential spies and military suppliers all are now required to be fingerprinted. Due to the nature of Colleen's alleged crime she becomes a person of interest in this criminal case, unfortunately. Otherwise, the Fourth Amendment restricts the use of fingerprint collection except for a reasonable identification. I hate seeing Colleen treated like a common criminal. However, this small town is not accustomed to murders and the law enforcement people are really running everything by the book. Maybe having Colleen's fingerprints might be more helpful to her than harmful. We shall see."

At that point, the judge entered the courtroom and the court was called to order. Colleen pleaded not guilty, and Mr. Wagner tried to get her released on recognizance. The male judge, who was rather thrilled to be in association with big city lawyers, absolutely refused. In fact, he set the bond so high it was just too expensive for anyone in that area to be able to afford getting Colleen out of jail. This order made the parents of Colleen extremely upset. The trial was set for approximately two weeks away.

Their daughter was removed from the courtroom to be returned to the jail, and Mrs. O'Conner nearly fainted again. Colleen's eyes met with her mother's and she had such a pleading look on her face that Doris had all she could do to keep from running to grab her daughter away from the men removing her.

Jack asked Mr. Wagner what was going to happen next. "Well, we will select a jury and prepare to defend your daughter. I just hope she is not withholding vital information from me that could help her."

This last statement worried Jack because he too had the feeling Colleen was not telling everything she knew. This matter was of great concern, and Jack wondered what could be so horrible that Colleen would not want to mention it. However, he did not get a lot of time to focus on the matter because his wife gave the impression that she might be ill. He put his arms around Doris and escorted her from the courtroom.

Jack's mother was helping in the store. Surprisingly, the elder Mrs. O'Conner was enjoying living here more than was ever expected. While she would have preferred being in the courtroom that day, she was needed in the store, so the need overtook her desires. Of course, she was concerned about her granddaughter and what all of this was doing to her family, but it was more than that. She felt a sort of need for living by being on the east coast. Her friends meant a lot to her, but in reality, nothing could take the place of being with family. While her husband was alive, she did not miss the family as much, but also, she never had the opportunity to meet them. Now, that opportunity was provided to her. The family filled her life with something special she was unaware she wanted or needed. Plus, their beauty and accomplishments made her proud to be a mother and grandmother. That was irreplaceable. She instinctively knew her granddaughter could not have committed that horrible crime of which she had been accused. Cora prayed every day that this would all come to a good end, and she pleaded it would be sooner rather than later.

When she saw the car return with her son and daughter-in-law, the senior Mrs. O'Conner indicated to the other person also working that she would leave for an hour or so to take care of Jack and Doris, but if she was needed, to please call. She started to make them lunch while listening to all that had occurred that morning at court.

Grandma thought for sure Colleen would be released from jail. She mentally wondered what good it was doing to keep an innocent teenager imprisoned. To her, Colleen was innocent. Grandma saw no point in pretending otherwise. Only, the court was not pretending. The town was almost thriving on the murder case. This little area had not experienced so much publicity in years. All the local stores were making money off the back of the teenager. Even the dry cleaner's business had increased. People wanted to make a good appearance for all the big city cameras, and out of towners used the cleaners to keep their own clothes in tip top shape. The nearest hotel was about a fifteen-minute drive away. It was not big city elegant, but it did have a charm about it that could not be denied. The décor was stylish, and, for the 1950's, it did not get much better unless you were in the city itself.

The hotel restaurant staff was overworked. People were calling room service all hours of the evening until the restaurant had to put a time limit of two in the early morning. In the past, eating late at night had not been an issue. The busy restaurant's workforce was not only over worked, they were also under paid. Friends were abusing their room privilege by calling for friends who stopped by just in the hope of having them order room service after the hotel restaurant closed. Nothing was opened at nighttime in those days except the local diner which did stay open later, but it too was way over crowded.

Homeowners were astounded by how much people were willing to pay to stay either in a room, or a converted bed and breakfast. So, of course they took advantage of the situation, and bed and breakfasts and room rentals were sprouting up all over town. The owners of these homes were filled with women who loved to cook and the people who stayed there had some of the best meals ever to include beef pot roasts and pies galore. One would have thought the town was enjoying a festival instead of a murder trial.

 In fact, Dr. & Mrs. Gelman were quite upset by the whole fiasco, even though the doctor also was bombarded by new patients. Several of their neighbors had opened their homes to the out-of-towners.

"It's disgraceful how everyone is trying to make money off the back of Colleen. That poor child." Mrs. Gelman was beside herself.

"I have mixed feelings about the whole process. Of course, I feel strange, since all of this is because our daughter's close friend has been accused of murder. However, we all like the opportunity to make extra money, so I do understand why our neighbors chose to do this." The voice of the more practical doctor interjected.

"I guess I can appreciate your point of view. I just cannot imagine what that poor family is going through. Even worse, I can't think of Colleen in jail without wanting to cry."

"I know honey. This whole thing is a mess. I only hope it turns out well. The best thing for us to do is go to bed and get some much-needed rest."

15

As predicted, the city attorneys wanted the trial held in another location claiming the town would be prejudiced in favor of Colleen. For most of the town this was probably true since they knew in their hearts this child was incapable of murder. There also was the smaller jealous element who thought otherwise. People can find any reason to be jealous.

They envied the parents having the business and bar. They envied the friendship of the three girls. Boys were unhappy because of their own bias of anyone so pretty and their own lack of self-esteem in thinking someone that pretty would never date them. Downright jealous were the girls who really did not know Colleen or her friends. Since they did not know them and the three girls were so pretty, they hated them without good reason. Given the opportunity to meet the girls and especially Colleen by joining a school club, etc., they easily found the girls were extremely well liked for a reason. The reason was because they were genuinely nice people. However, some girls wanted nothing to do with school clubs, so they were unlikely ever to meet. It was this group of people who had hatred in their hearts and were looking for any reason at all to condemn Colleen. If it were up to them though they would never move the trial to another town. Their intentions were to spend every spare minute in the courtroom watching the trial.

Mr. Wagner tried his best to convince the Judge that the trial should stay right here in town. Among the more valid reasons was the frivolous motive to keep Colleen close to her parents as an innocent child should be. The Judge was not so convinced of Colleen's innocence, but he attempted to be fair by listening to both sides state their case. What he did not say was that there was no way they were going to move this case to another town. He personally enjoyed the publicity, and the town itself was thriving because of the trial. In the end, as professional as the Judge should be, he presented his ruling for keeping the trial in the area, and that was that. Mr. Wagner was on the phone immediately to the O'Conners.

"Well, we won that round," he told them. "The trial will remain in town."

"Oh, super," exclaimed Doris. "What happens now?"

"Now, comes the jury selection. That might not come out in our favor, unfortunately."

"Why?"

"The other side is not going to want any juror who knows your family. Since you own a business that is going to present some problems. Heck, everyone is this town knows everyone else."

This was just another reason for Doris to worry, but Mr. Wagner had a way of anticipating any worry the family might have, and he was prepared with his calm manner to put them at ease.

* * *

The murder was the talk of the town. It consumed everybody. Roy and Rabbit were no different even though the two of them had a love/hate relationship with one another. Despite their off and on relationship, the two seemed made for each other and being pals together just seemed to fit them.

"I'm mad that the people think my Colleen committed murder. She's too sweet and definitely too pretty to do such a thing."

"Being pretty has nothing to do with it. Pretty people murder too."

"You know Rabbit, if it hadn't been for Colleen's friend Barbara, I might have died after you pushed me in the gulley."

"Well, watch what you say to me in the future."

"What did I say that was so bad?"

"If you can't remember, you can't expect me to remember. All I know is it made me very angry. I ain't never going to let people put me down. My Mom says it's not right."

"Which Mom? You don't even know who your Mom is for crying out loud."

"It doesn't matter, so don't you say no more about that. Somebody told me it's not right, and I believe it."

"I'm sorry Rabbit. You are right, we should never say bad things about other people. Though whoever really killed Margie should be big and say they did it, so my Colleen won't have to be in jail no more."

Rabbit didn't say anything about that because he was giving Roy's statement a lot of thought.

The two boys were walking through town and waving to people they knew. Roy did say, "Lordy, I never seen so many people in this small town."

"Yea, we ought to figure a way to make money off them. Everybody else seems to be doing it."

They walked into the ice cream parlor and each bought an ice cream cone. One chose a sugar cone with cherry vanilla ice cream, and the other got a cake cone with chocolate ice cream. They noticed the newspapers on the rack and saw the headlines with a picture of Colleen. "I wish I had enough money to buy the paper. Then, I could cut out Miss Colleen's picture and hang it in my room."

"You lucky. You got a room."

Roy contemplated each word that just came out of his friend's mouth. "What's it like Rabbit, going from house to house and sometimes sleeping out under the stars?"

"It's not so bad. Especially when the weather is nice. Many of the homes on Park Avenue have two outside slanted doors that open to house cellars. They are kind of dirty inside, but it's a good place for me to stay. One place in particular, I've stayed there so long that I have a makeshift bed with sheets and blankets that I stole off a lady's clothes line."

"No joke?" Roy was in awe.

"That's right. Other nights those families on Park Avenue have so many kids they don't even know when an extra one is hanging around."

Roy stamped his feet and said, "I'll be damned." He thought it was all kind of neat. Of course, Roy should talk. His Mom was so busy joining, doing or sewing for other people that he was left alone a good majority of the time to do as he pleased.

"Let's write a note for Colleen and leave it in her mailbox so's the mom and dad can take it to her."

"Who's going to walk up on her porch and put it in the mailbox? I sure ain't going to do it," said Rabbit.

By this time the boys were near Roy's house on Park Avenue. He ran in and wrote the note while Rabbit waited outside. "I signed your name too Rabbit."

"I hope my name don't get me in trouble."

"Don't be silly. I'll run up the porch and slip it in the mailbox. Be prepared to run fast when I get back down until we are several blocks away." They ran in the opposite direction of Roy's house and noticed a funeral parlor. "Let's go in and see if there are any dead people."

"God, Roy, you must be nuts. I don't wanna see no dead people."

"Oh, come on." The house door was open as the boys slid in quietly. There was a stand with prayer cards, and they each took one and walked to the room where they saw a coffin. A man's body was lying there. Flowers were spread about the coffin and two lamps were lit, one on each side of the body to the right and to the left side. Roy touched the body and Rabbit screeched, so both boys turned around and ran out into the street.

"I don't wanna see any more dead people. I seen enough of them by now."

"What do you mean you seen enough. You didn't even touch him."

By then they each saw a stone on the sidewalk and started having a race as to who could kick it further.

"Someday, I'm going to tell you a big secret Roy."

"Tell me now."

"Nope, I can't."

"Who says so. You know I'm going to bug you every day until you tell me."

They passed a field where some of the boys were playing football and their conversation stopped as they decided to join the game. Thoughts of Colleen were temporarily forgotten.

16

The opposing side had no trouble picking jurors. Many were quite willing to get their fifteen minutes of fame and chastise one of the town's favorite daughters. Mr. Wagner, on the other hand, was having a most difficult time. Most who knew the family had no intention of being a juror. They wanted no part in being remembered as those individuals who may have found Colleen guilty. With persistence, the family's attorney was able to finally come up with what he felt were respectable and fair jurors. The total comprised two older men, an older woman and some teenagers who were in their late teens, lived in the area but ran with a different crowd. They seemed stable and without an agenda which was in Colleen's favor.

For all intents and purposes, it appeared that everything was settled, and the case was ready to be tried in court.

No one, however, knew of what was occurring in the big city apartment of Mr. and Mrs. Chapman.

"We don't know if Colleen is aware of our daughter's sexual preferences," stated the Mrs.

"I guess we'll just have to wait and see and hope for the best."

"I don't want that type of information spread all over the news."

"Well, it isn't as though we have a lot of choice in the matter."

"Then we just have to think of something."

Mr. Chapman was getting annoyed with his wife. Here they had lost their daughter and she was worried about how everyone would take the news that their daughter was gay. What the hell difference did it make anyway? Yet, the last thing he wanted to do was get in a fight over the matter with his wife.

"What on earth do you suggest?" He was beside himself with remorse for his lost child.

"I don't know, damn it."

"You'll have to do better than that babe. You can't show concern without having some type of solution."

"Well, we are husband and wife. Can't you even discuss the matter with me? Offer me some solutions as to what you think we might do."

"I'm willing to go to court and hopefully put the person in jail who murdered our daughter."

"You don't really think that darling Colleen murdered Margie, do you?"

"Damn it. I don't know. I would like to think not, but then if she didn't do it, who did? Can you answer that for me?"

"The only way I sometimes think she murdered Margie is when I think perhaps Margie may have made some advances toward Colleen which repulsed her. So far, no one has ever mentioned that fact. But then again, why would you murder someone for that? You would push them away and perhaps not befriend them anymore."

"God, you are really going overboard now. Our daughter may have liked other girls, but make advances toward them? You've got to be kidding."

"Gosh, I'm trying to examine this thing from all angles. Give me a break here and try to think of a solution. I don't want our daughter's name smeared all over the news."

"Hey, as you were saying that, I think I may have come up with something."

"Really?"

"Why don't we offer them a settlement. If they accept, we won't even have to go to trial."

"What's a settlement?"

"We would have to give them a rather large sum of money to close the case. And, they would have to accept it."

"How large a sum?"

"Extravagant is the only word I can think of. After all, you must take into consideration what the whole family has gone through, and what it has done to their daughter's reputation."

"What about what we've gone through? Are we mincemeat?"

"Come on Babe. You asked for a solution, and I'm trying to give you one. No one would even consider a small amount of money. In fact, they might not even want a lot of money."

"I've never known anyone to turn down large sums of money, regardless of the reason."

"You are talking about people in business. Sometimes, in the private lives of individuals, people's reputations mean more than any excessive amounts of cash."

"Do you think your idea is a good one?"

"Unless you can come up with one better, then yes I do. Please know though that I am only doing this because of your concerns. However, the more I think that we might not have to go through the process of having a trial, the more I approve of your idea."

"What's the next step?"

"I guess the best thing to do is call our lawyer. He can help us come up with a reasonable amount of money to offer the family while also giving us the proper procedure of how to go about making the offer. While the O'Conner family owns a business, I cannot see them turning away a lot of money. Also, they won't have to go through a trial."

"Will you do that for us in the morning? It is rather late now and we need to get some rest. The masseuse is coming here tomorrow. Hopefully, I can get some release for the bodily tension I've been feeling. Then later in the day my hairdresser is coming."

"How did you manage all this when you were going to work every day?"

"They just came to the office instead of my house. It does seem women require more maintenance than men to keep them looking good, but hey, I run a company and can do as I please, just like you run your company as you please."

"I can't deny that Babe." They started walking around the room turning out lights. Tomorrow was going to be a busy day and they were both hopeful of the outcome of the choices they had made.

17

Having called a meeting of all the employees, John was in the bar before it opened. The hope was to make a schedule to cover his absence during the trial. Expectations were high that a good majority of the town intended to be at the trial and that business would be slow. Doris was back at the house helping her mother-in-law clean the breakfast dishes. The cheery kitchen with the sun peeping through the pale-yellow ruffled curtains defied the mood inside. The phone rang startling both women.

Mr. Wagner was on the line. Knowing that busy body neighbors liked to listen in on the party lines, he made an appointment to see them later in the day.

"Is everything ok with Colleen?"

"Yes, she's fine. I just have something I need to discuss with you and your husband."

"Can you come around five o'clock? That is usually when Jack comes back to the house for a few hours before heading back to handle the busy evenings in the bar."

"Five should be fine. I'll see you then."

The mother-in-law looked at Doris inquisitively.

"That was the lawyer Ma. He's coming to see both of us at five tonight.

I'm sure what he has to say you can hear too though. We are all in this together."

Doris began to grasp how her mother-in-law was indeed an angel in disguise. She did not realize she could love someone so much that she had just met. To think back to the day when she heard her mother-in-law was coming, she almost felt it was going to be more of a hindrance. However, it turned out not to be a burden at all. Doris could see where her husband got his good looks and often the two women would sit and talk really about nothing for hours. This was a skill that Jack never acquired, and it soothed the very soul of Doris. Not only was Cora's companionship a blessing, but she was not the type of person to sit around being waited on. Instead, often she did more than her share because Doris just sat there in a stupor. Doris thanked God everyday for having met her mother-in-law and for the fact that she was such a pleasure to be near.

The conversation that day mostly was about wondering why their attorney wanted to see them.

"Maybe he just wants to go over again dear what is going to happen when Colleen goes to court."

"Yea, I guess it could be that. This waiting all day drives me crazy."

The day managed to progress pretty fast, and Jack came in from the bar area about ten minutes to five o'clock. He grabbed a few things out of the refrigerator to satisfy his hunger and sat down in the living room to talk to his Mother and Doris. Jack's bottom no longer reached the chair when there was a knock on the front door. Jack got immediately up again to answer the door and was happy to see Mr. Wagner.

* * *

Doris pointed to a chair nearby and offered the attorney a seat. He fiddled in his brief case for something after seating himself. "It feels good to sit down. I've been on the go all day."

"Let me get you a cup of coffee before we start." Doris had already started towards the kitchen. "That is unless you prefer something else to drink?"

"Actually, coffee would be great. Thank you." He noticed the cheese and fruit platter Doris had already put on the coffee table, and he helped himself to a few pieces of each. This was the first time he had the opportunity to look the room over, and he noticed that the décor was already set up for spring as though they had already done spring cleaning. Tasteful floral slipcovers adorned the couch and one chair, and the curtains at the windows were light and airy as opposed to the heavy winter drapes still in some homes. While the home was modest in appearance, it was obvious to someone with knowledge that the mahogany furniture was of a good quality. At that point, the senior Mrs. O'Conner came in the room with a pot of coffee, while Doris also brought in cold glasses of water along with the cream and sugar.

Mr. Wagner stood when the women entered the room and was told politely that standing was not necessary. He fixed his coffee, took a swallow and told Doris that her cheese and fruit platter and delicious coffee hit the spot. Jack also helped himself to some of the goodies and fixed himself some coffee too.

"I have a bit of surprise offer for you which could keep Colleen from having to go to trial. This type of offer is most unusual in a murder case."

All three of Colleen's relatives looked up when the attorney made his statement.

"I have yet to figure out why this is happening to tell you the truth."

The trio became even more suspicious.

Finally, Jack said, "Well, what is the offer that you think is so strange?"

The Chapman's want to settle the case right now and not go to court. They have offered you more money than I personally ever had to experience, and believe me I've handled some large corporate settlements. Of course, if you say yes, a settlement attorney will handle the process.

When all in the family heard the amount, they were completely astonished, and Doris, who had been standing, immediately sat down flabbergasted.

"Wow, why would they do that?"

"I've been just as puzzled about this as anyone else. The only thing I can come up with is that they must be trying to hide something. What it could possibly be floors me. I just have no idea. However, it does mean you would never have to go to court."

"In that case, I think we should take the offer," said Jack.

"No way, our daughter is not guilty," exclaimed Doris.

The two men looked at Doris as though she were crazy. Grandma just sat in her chair with an astonished look on her face.

Finally, the attorney said, "Mr. and Mrs. O'Conner. I can't guarantee your daughter will be set free as hard as I will try to do so. You have to know that, or I can't continue representing Colleen."

"I just feel we will be remiss if we don't try."

Jack was more adamant saying, "With that amount of money, we could sell everything here and move to Missouri to be with Mom. We don't really have to worry what the hell anyone thinks about Colleen. We'll just move away."

"What do you think Mr. Wagner?"

"I have mixed feelings. Certainly, with that amount of money your whole quality of life will be changed. I can't even imagine myself in your position right now."

"Money itself is not what makes people happy. I don't want to go to my grave thinking we did not try to exonerate Colleen." Doris was almost in tears.

"You heard what our attorney said. Colleen may be innocent, but we can't know if the jury will find her that way."

All of a sudden, Jack looked at his mother. "Ma, what would you do if you were us?"

"Children, first of all, I am not you. Right now, I can see the reasons both of you are thinking the way you do. But, if you want my opinion, this is what I think I would do. There is no doubt in my mind we have to go to court. My sweet granddaughter needs to go through the process and hopefully get her name freed."

Jack countered, "Even if she is set free, there will always be an element of the population who will continue to think she did it regardless."

"That's very true dear, but she will not have it on her record to deal with the rest of her life."

"If we move away, no one will even care."

"Jack, you are not thinking right. Colleen may want to go to college or apply for a government job. If she has this mark on her record, she may not be accepted or hired."

Clutching his hands behind his head with his elbows pointing out like two sticks put there to brace his cranium, Jack started pacing the room - back and forth, back and forth.

Mr. Wagner grabbed a sip of coffee, while Doris sat there crying.

Grandma finally asked the lawyer if they needed to give him an answer right that minute.

He explained he could wait until tomorrow, but he needed to know by then if the trial was to continue, or not. He picked up his briefcase and started to leave.

Jack stopped him by saying, "Tell those damn city people they can't buy us with money. We do not accept their offer. I sure would like to know why they made the stupid offer in the first place."

"Actually, so would I, as it could help me in defending your daughter. I'll give them your answer tomorrow. By the way, my daughter Mia and Barbara are going to testify for Colleen. We are grabbing for straws here though because neither one of them was with Colleen the day of the murder. That is part of the problem. Those few minutes your daughter went to the bathroom and then left it on her own create more problems than I care to admit. However, the girls will testify about Colleen's character and her state of mind the day prior to the incident. One of my assistants will be questioning my daughter."

Doris escorted Mr. Wagner to the door and stood behind the screen door watching him drive away. She also could notice some neighbors peeking through their curtains. Those on the street just downright stopped their conversations to look. Doris mentally said to herself, "My God, are we making the right decision?"

"I've got dinner ready in the oven," said Grandma, the practical one. "Jack needs to eat before he goes back to work. We all need to eat to keep ourselves healthy. These next few weeks are going to try our patience more than we might want to admit."

Each of them grabbed something or other to progress with the meal, and they sat down asking for God's grace and thanking him for the food they were about to eat.

18

The Chapman's were seated at their dining room table eating breakfast which was more like a feast. A sideboard was filled with enough food to feed an army. Each ate an egg out of individual egg holders often seen in Europe, when the phone rang.

The butler walked to the end table to take the phone off the receiver. "Chapman Residence." Both Chapmans turned their heads and quieted their conversation to listen to what was being said.

The butler grabbed the phone and handed it to the Mister. Covering the mouthpiece so as not to be heard, the butler said. "It's the accused's attorney."

"Hi Mr. Wagner." Mr. Chapman was ecstatic. He was sure the O'Conner's had accepted their monetary offer. "Everything go well?"

"Actually, no. They want the case to go to trial. I contacted your attorney, and he asked me if I wanted to call you. While it is completely out of character for me to call you, I accepted his offer."

When Mrs. Chapman saw the strange look on her husband's face, she took her napkin off her lap, set it on the table and stood up by her husband as though that were going to somehow make things better.

"What do you mean they won't accept the money? Do they want more?"

"No, they do not want any more money. What you offered was quite generous."

"Well, who would be stupid enough to turn down the offer?"

"I wouldn't call them stupid at all sir. In fact, I would advise you to not disparage the parents of Colleen in anyway. They maintain their daughter's innocence and are willing to go to court to prove that."

Mr. Chapman was furious, handed the phone to his wife, and started walking around the room swearing. Emily gripped her hand over the mouthpiece and told her husband to shut up.

Finally, she said, "Hello, what's up? Something has made my husband very angry."

"The bottom-line Mrs. Chapman is what I already told your husband. The O'Conner family has turned down your monetary offer."

"Why? What do they know that we don't?"

"Well, I could ask you the same thing. What do you know that we don't?"

"Mr. Wagner, we are not playing games. That was a very generous offer."

"It was very generous, but Doris and Jack are not interested. So, I'll see you in court. Do you have any more questions for me before I terminate this call?"

"No ahh no..." At this point the attorney had already hung up and Mrs. Chapman held the phone in her hand and looked at it as though the caller would return.

The butler discreetly left the room. He could envision an explosion coming. The two Chapmans could have a good fight under normal circumstances. He did not want to be in the room for this one, as he could foresee things getting thrown around the room and broken. They seemed never to be concerned about destroying things that he knew were valuable.

This time though, the two Chapmans appeared depleted and defeated. That was their last hope, and it fell through. "God only knows now what is going to come out."

"Please don't be concerned about that. So, our daughter was gay. She was still beautiful, and now she is gone. I just don't care what comes out. Who cares?"

"Oh honey, I still care. I don't want negative things to spread around for the gossips. They will thrive on it." At that, the two individuals had walked toward each other and embraced, but their embrace was one of defeat. The prosecuting attorney called at that time. Normally, the parents of the deceased would have met with both attorneys to be told that the O'Conner's refused monetary help. However, when Mr. Wagner was asked by the prosecutor if he would like to talk to the family, he agreed. Since the whole scenario was highly unusual anyway, Mr. Wagner followed up with a phone call to the Chapmans soon after.

The maid had just returned to the kitchen from the second floor of the home where she cleaned the Master Bedroom and changed the sheets on the bed, a daily ritual. She saw the butler in the kitchen and asked what he was doing there.

"I wanted to be out of the dining room. I expected there was going to be a big fight between the two of them as so often happens, but they completely surprised me."

"What would they be fighting about now for heaven's sake."

"The family of the girl accused of murdering our Margie refused a financial settlement from what I could gather."

"That's so typical of the Chapman's. Money, money, money. They have it and think everybody else wants to be like them. When will they ever learn?"

"I heard it was a big fat sum. I don't think I could personally turn it down."

"You are as bad as the two of them. When are you going to learn that money can't buy respect, honor or make you part of the esteemed population?"

"Maybe you have never been poor."

"Most of us go to work everyday just to get by. We work hard, and if we did not work, we would be poor. Not all of us are born with a silver spoon in our mouth."

"That's exactly my point. I don't want to go to work every day. If the Chapman's offered me a big chunk of money today, I would take it and run."

"You are just like the rest of them. Remember this, money can't buy you happiness."

"Well, I sure would like to have it and be unhappy for a while."

"Pffft," said the maid and dismissed him as she went about her chores in another room.

In the meantime, Mrs. Chapman had recovered enough that she immediately changed her tone by saying, "I need to go shopping today to get some outfits to wear to court."

"Oh my God. You have a closet full of clothes that no one has ever seen. In fact, I am not sure I have even seen you wear them. Sometimes, I think you just like to spend money for the sake of spending it."

The Mrs. gave her husband no attention and continued with her plans to shop.

19

Mr. Wagner once again attempted to talk with Colleen in the hope he could bring out what she seemed to be withholding. He mentally thought to himself that jail had not taken away the child's beauty. In reality, she was closer in age to an adult than a child. While the jail in this small town was unisex, efforts were made as much as possible to keep the women and men separate. Most of the women who came to jail were prostitutes. It was extremely rare to have a woman admitted for murdering someone. Colleen was of a different character than most who were confined, but she made the utmost of a life in jail by adjusting and offering to help the very few others who were incarcerated. She instructed one woman in how to read and tutored the two other women in helping them get a General Education Diploma. The GED was relatively new at the time having started a few years before in 1942, and to some it was called General Education Development, but the results were the same.

"Hi Colleen. I want to go over your testimony with you. I also want you to remember that the prosecution is not going to be friendly to you. In fact, many times they will be downright insulting and harsh. Do you think you want to take the stand and endure what some might consider abuse?"

"I think if I just tell the truth, that will be most important to everybody."

Mr. Wagner could see that Colleen really did not understand the process. She was too sweet and innocent in her behavior. He still did not know if putting her on the stand was wise. He did feel the need to practice with her just in case.

"Let's go back to that awful day. You were already in the girls' room when Margie came in and saw you?"

"That's right sir."

"What did you talk about?"

"Just general topics."

"Well, what caused you to get mad at her?"

"I don't remember."

"That type of answer is not going to sit well with the other attorneys. Something made you mad. What was it?"

"I don't know. Maybe she was fixing something on my dress, and I didn't want her to do that."

"Was that enough to get you mad at her?"

Colleen didn't answer.

"The girls on the cheerleading squad said the two of you were fighting."

"I wouldn't call it that."

"What would you call it? The prosecutors are going to be putting some of the squad on the stand."

"I would not say we were fighting. We were just discussing something."

"What were you discussing?"

"I don't remember."

"Colleen, I won't deny I am getting extremely frustrated with you. From day one I have felt you were keeping information from me, and that is just not good. I can't help you 100% if you are not going to tell me the truth."

"I'm not really lying sir."

"If you are not REALLY lying, just what would you call it?"

Again, Colleen just sat there without saying anything.

"Whatever it is child that you are not telling me could be the one thing that might help me win this case. I have to go now, but I really hope you consider everything I've told you today and be more forthcoming with me in the future."

"Yes sir!"

The attorney left and Colleen was alone in her cell for a while. She slumped over in desperation. How could she tell everyone that Margie made advances to her? I'll be the laughingstock of the town. No one will ever believe me. Her thoughts wandered all over the place and she finally said a silent prayer. Oh God, please help me. Give me some sign of what you would like me to do, please?

It was outside recreation time by then. This was the one time of the day Colleen enjoyed the most. She especially liked to be outdoors when the weather was nice.

* * *

The trial was to start the next day. Groups of people were coming in from the city. The latest model cars were driving up and down Main Boulevard and Center Street.

There was a fancy resort about thirty minutes away where most of the people stayed. The whole scenario was like a vacation to some. The people who stayed at the resort were called the celebrities though they really were not. The others stayed at the hastily formed bed and breakfasts right in the town, or the rather close hotel in town. The celebrities got that name because anyone who could afford the fancy resort had to be a celebrity in the minds of the town folk. Men always wore suits and the men and women had designer clothes. The town people were secretly enjoying the entire spectacle even if the reason for it was not a good one.

As already explained earlier, those individuals that stayed at the bed and breakfasts were treated daily to feasts beyond the imagination. The owners went out and bought new pillows and sheet sets, and some even gave the rooms a fresh coat of paint. They were proud to host the city dwellers, and they wanted bragging rights when the trial was over, and the people returned to the city.

Many journalists wrote about their adventures in the city newspapers and gave their hosts a copy of the printed materials. Often, after being asked for permission to do so, the owners could see their name in print, and that made them extremely proud.

The few local restaurants in existence in the small town were overcrowded with lines often out the door and sometimes blocks long. Because most of the establishments were extremely busy, the O'Conner bar also saw an upbeat in customers. When those who lived in the town saw the places on Main Boulevard over-crowded, the town people chose to go to the O'Conner bar which was off the beaten path and not as familiar to outsiders. Sad to say, but it was true, that the O'Conner family also profited by their own daughter being on trial.

That summer evening the two women in the O'Conner household decided to enjoy the pleasant weather by sitting in their back yard. Doris missed talking to her daughter, but she did have to admit that the older

Colleen got she was not always present, as she often was out with her friends. Having her mother-in-law there to enjoy a pleasant conversation was indeed the right medicine while Jack was working.

"I was walking through town this afternoon after stopping to see Colleen. The whole structure of the town has changed tremendously. Fancy cars drive up and down the streets. God only knows where they are going. Some of the locals that converted their homes to bed and breakfasts must have also mentioned to the outsiders about the two lakes. I understand the two small public areas for swimming were so crowded that those who live here decided to go on home. Of course, the locals know of the private areas where they can go too, so that was a plus for them."

"How did you find that out Ma?"

"I met Mrs. Wagner in passing on the street, and we stopped and talked a little. We started out by talking about the traffic which almost made you fear crossing the street."

"How was Colleen doing?"

"She looks remarkably well considering...though I still get the feeling expressed by Mr. Wagner. Colleen is withholding vital information that could possibly help her case. Mrs. Wagner said her husband tried to get Barbara and Mia to go and perhaps get the information out of her. Unfortunately, they could not do the job either."

"I hope we made the right choice in turning down the money from the Chapmans. The closer we get to trial, the more worried I get."

"Don't second guess yourself Doris. It's in the hands of the attorney and God now. Have faith that all will turn out well."

"You're right. At least I have you here to bounce off my fears. Do you realize what a blessing you've become?"

"Now, now. No need to praise me. We can save all the praise for when Colleen is freed."

"Amen to that!"

"Oh, by the way. Mrs. Wagner told me her husband said the Chapmans were beside themselves when they heard you wouldn't accept their monetary offer. He almost got some pleasure telling them you had turned it down."

"No joke? I guess some of those types of people think that people like us can be bought off. Well, they think wrong."

"Yes dear, they did. Good for you." Around that time the mosquitos were out to get them, and the two women went inside since it was late anyway.

20

Today was court day. The weather was sunny and clear. Doris could not decide if that were a good or bad omen. She too had paid attention to what she wore but for different reasons than Mrs. Chapman who wanted to be noticed first and foremost. Doris would have gladly preferred not to be noticed at all. However, on the supposition everyone might be examining the mother and father of the convicted person she wanted to look presentable without being ostentatious.

Doris had purchased a pale blue suit from the Sears Roebuck catalogue. She purposely picked light blue instead of navy blue or black. It was hot out and she felt no need to look like a dull winter had hit her. The light blue was summery and cooler to wear. She knew the courtroom would get hot with only a few overhead fans and some floor fans stuck around the room to ease the in-room temperatures. The light color also went well with the soft red curls that framed Mrs. O'Conner's head. She was a beauty just like her daughter and when she walked down that aisle to her seat, she intended to flaunt that fact. No one in that courtroom was going to feel sorry for poor Mrs. O'Conner. Jack had also purchased a dark, navy blue suit from the same catalogue. The two were a handsome couple for sure which made the elder Mrs. O'Conner look at them with pride.

Grandma always managed to look nice as she chose the dress she wore to her husband's funeral. That sad day, a large portion of the dress she wore had been covered by a coat, but today no coat was needed. The dress accented Grandma's tiny waist with a navy-blue belt to match the material on the dress which had a white collar that broke up the moroseness of the otherwise dark dress.

The trio was kept in an alternate room out of sight of everyone. This same consideration was given to the Chapmans who were placed in a different room. A few snacks were provided in each of the rooms along with pitchers of ice-cold water. People concerned about getting a seat, or even getting in the courtroom, started coming early in the day for the one o'clock in the afternoon proceeding.

Roy and Rabbit had no intention of missing any of it. They snuck to the nosebleed section way up in the balcony. Up in that sector, they figured they would not be asked to give up their seats to someone more prominent. They could barely see over the railing, but with well-placed speakers, they surely could hear all that transpired.

The black highly expensive suit Mrs. Chapman chose to wear that day with white piping fit her figure to perfection. With her now short coiffed bleached blonde hair she was a specimen to behold. Her husband also wore a black designer suit and they came across as a city power couple – which they were.

Both attorneys entered the building around the same time pushing themselves through the crowds that had also gathered early for several blocks outside the courtroom. To be more exact, their assistants were pushing the crowds away from the two men. Many of the outsiders had signs saying FREE COLLEEN. Unfortunately, there were also some signs saying COLLEEN – MURDERER though some had spelled murderer wrong.

The seating turned out to be somewhat like a wedding. All the city dwellers sat on the side of the prosecutor, and the town folk sat behind the defense. Designer clothes aside, the town women gave the designer crowd a run for their money. While the city women were extremely svelte in their designer outfits and perfectly styled hair, the local women somehow managed to outdo those from the metropolitan area. First, they were slim, but curved in all the right places, some might even call them voluptuous. Their outfits either came from local dress shops or from one of the catalogs. While their clothes might not have had designer labels, those women were used to wearing smart outfits whether to church, parties or stores, and therefore they knew exactly how to present themselves. Never having had facial uplifts or other types of surgery, they had a natural beauty that caused many from the city area to be envious.

The only ones in town that knew Colleen and did not come that day were Dr. & Mrs. Gelman. The doctor had patients scheduled the entire week and being one of only two doctors in the vicinity, duty called. Since Mrs. Gelman worked for her husband, no one even questioned their absence. Mrs. Wagner was there to give her husband, her daughter Mia and Barbara support along with the O'Conner family.

Noise in the courtroom reached a crescendo that was almost out of control. The sound diminished greatly as the bailiff called the court to order and asked everyone in the court to rise when Judge Stallone entered the courtroom and sat down. Once everything was settled, The Honorable Judge then asked the attorneys for each side of the case if they were ready to begin the trial. The "circus" was about to begin.

* * *

The Coroner had already stated that Margaret had a direct blow to the back of her head. Mr. Wagner, on cross examination, questioned the Coroner on if Colleen had the strength to create such a blow, and he also queried as to what could be the instrument that Colleen used to do this? No instrument had yet been found. This was one thing in Colleen's favor. No object could be found to confirm the prosecutor's suspicions. Yet, Colleen was charged with pre-meditated murder. The cross-exam proved very effective for the defense.

One of the other witnesses to be questioned was the person who found the body in the woods behind the girls' rest room. That really did not prove much where Colleen was concerned. Many wondered how Colleen could get the body from the rest room to the wooded area. Then it was time for the girls' junior varsity cheerleading squad to be queried.

Each one got up separately to give their statement and things did not look good.

When the judge called a recess, Roy and Rabbit left the courtroom, and grabbed their bikes. With the lunches Roy's mother made that morning for both boys, they took off for one of their favorite areas. The lunches had been kept in the bikes' baskets. They drove about five minutes away to one of the lakes where they were going to skim small rocks and larger stones across the water.

Rabbit was the first to open his lunch. Most of the school year no one bothered to feed Rabbit and he grabbed what he could from friends and families like Roy's. Inside the sack he had peanut butter and jelly sandwiches, some cookies, sliced oranges, a banana and peanuts in shells. The bread had been homemade by Roy's mother who did not want to give them anything that would spoil in the heat. While in court, the boys found a nice shady spot to leave their bikes in a private area that no one seemed to know about except Rabbit, so as it turned out the lunches were kept nice and cool. All the food was packed in the new plastic containers Roy's mother had just purchased at a new type of home selling party where the person demonstrating showed the proper way to operate the lids in order to open and close them properly. Roy had to promise his mother to return the containers. He was used to throwing away paper bags that used to hold his lunches before these plastic holders became the "in" thing, and he did not much like having to worry about bringing the receptacles home.

"Your Mom makes the best bread of anyone I know," said Rabbit as he almost gulped the sandwich down in one big bite.

"Yup," answered Roy. "My favorite thing to do when I come home from school is smear the bread in butter and put lots of sugar on it. Hmm, hmm, now that's what I call good."

"Hey, brother, you are not telling me anything new, as I practically go home with you every day during the school year."

"True, you are the one guy who knows what I mean."

They both stretched themselves and sat down on the ground. For a long time neither boy said anything, each deep in their own thoughts. Roy noticed that Rabbit's demeanor was different than normal. He finally said to him, "What's up Rabbit? You're acting strange."

"Those cheerleaders really were nasty about Colleen. They made it sound like she for sure did it, and I don't think that's nice."

"Yea, I thought so too. I was looking at the faces of those on the jury to see if I could make out what they were thinking."

"Do you think we should go back now?"

Roy did not really answer, but instead started gathering everything to put in his bike's basket as though getting ready to leave.

Rabbit followed close behind.

* * *

The questioning of the cheerleaders had been brutal that session, or at least their responses were. The replies even gave Mr. Wagner's team concern. Every single girl had their own interpretation of what they called a fight.

Lois was the first to be questioned. She exclaimed that when their group walked in the girls' room, they saw Colleen pushing Margaret Chapman hard. "The two girls were fighting," she said.

When the prosecutor asked Lois another question concerning the fight, Mr. Wagner objected. No one could confirm the girls had been fighting, and the Judge agreed. However, the idea had now been planted in the minds of the jurors.

A lot of banter went back and forth concerning the "push away" that the cheerleading squad called a fighting move. So, that afternoon when court was back in session, Mr. Wagner felt it might be better not to cross examine the girls as they appeared to be very set in their ways. He felt that there was no chance in Hell he was going to change their minds. Plus, it was always at this point where Colleen clammed up by refusing to talk. This left Mr. Wagner in a horrible predicament because he knew Colleen was withholding pertinent information. Yet, that was the one and only place where he could not get Colleen to talk, and his frustration was starting to get the best of him.

During the court's recess, and before lunch, Mr. Wagner once again attempted to get Colleen to talk. He used the guise of practicing going over what had occurred once again. "You went to the girls' room from the classroom where you had been working on the yearbook. Correct?"

"Yes sir."

"Did all those working see you leave?"

"Most of them did. Yes sir."

"What happened when you got to the girls' room where Margie was concerned?"

"Margie was washing her hands sir, when I walked in. She came up to talk to me."

"What did you talk about?"

"I honestly don't remember."

Mr. Wagner took a deep breath, "What happened that caused you to shove Margie."

"I don't know why I shoved Margie."

"You must have had a reason, Colleen. You don't normally go around shoving people, do you?"

"No, sir."

"If you don't tell me what happened between the two of you, then you are making it extremely hard for me to defend you."

"One thing I know sir, I did not kill Margie. She was my friend."

"Why then, did you push her away from you?"

Colleen broke down in tears which could not have been more upsetting to Mr. Wagner. He became spineless when Mia cried, or his wife, and he was no better now. Colleen was like a second daughter. He was putty in Colleen's hands as her tears easily influenced him to terminate the questioning.

"Did you walk with Margie to the wooded area that is located behind the rest rooms?"

"No sir. I did not leave the room with Margie. Several people saw me walking back to the yearbook room through the corridors in school."

"Yes, I have several willing to attest to your state of being when you returned to the yearbook room. Though, I can find no one to confirm the time.

"I was very upset sir."

"I know Colleen, but you won't tell me what upset you. Afterall, you don't normally get upset after meeting friends in either the girls' room or the corridors for that matter."

Colleen just shrugged her shoulders.

He released Colleen to the guards to go and have some lunch at that point and called in his staff.

One young assistant said, "If Colleen left the girls' room and went straight back to the yearbook room, how would she have gotten Margie's body to the wooded area?"

"That's the one thing that is in Colleen's favor."

21

Mr. Wagner went home that night exhausted. He was filled with despair as it became more apparent the case for Colleen was very weak. His wife saw the worry on his face and was happy she had made a hearty dinner. The custom was for the whole family to sit around the dining room table every night at dinner time. Conversation was encouraged, and it was a good place to let off steam.

Tom removed his jacket and tie after kissing his wife and hugging his daughters. "This is the best part of my day where I get to come home and unwind." He grabbed his wife around the waist and told her whatever she was making it just smelled so darn good. "You do this every single night. To me you are a jewel a thousand times over the ritziest diamonds." Tom was always generous with his compliments, and he was rewarded in more ways than one.

They all said grace and family style eating began. "How did it go in court today honey?"

"Frankly, not so good. You were there, you tell me what you think of how it went?"

"I was just so nervous, I had all I could do to remain there."

"Don't be nervous dear. It is what it is. Mia can get up there and reiterate Colleen's good points, but she was not there when it happened. In fact, she did not even stay after school that day. None of the witnesses I have talking about Colleen's character were even there. My one hope is the boy who walked her home. My case is weak."

Mia popped up, "Yes, those girls on the cheerleading junior varsity squad were brutal today and very believable. Yet, none of what they said makes sense to me as her longtime friend. It just isn't in Colleen's nature to be confrontational, especially to another friend. Something is drastically missing."

"I feel the same way honey. I have felt that way from day one that Colleen is withholding important information, but I've given up trying to get it out of her. Can you please pass the rolls?"

"Funny thing Dad, Colleen just isn't the type to withhold anything. She is very straight forward and tells it like it is. None of this makes sense."

The mother had gotten up to get something from the kitchen and returned at that point. "I heard what you said about Colleen always being straight forward and honest. I have always liked that part of her disposition. What are you going to do?"

"I'm baffled for sure. Also, I feel incompetent – like I am going to lose this case and Colleen will be found guilty of murder."

"Oh, Blessed God," said Mrs. Wagner.

Mia's younger sister was taking it all in and listening intently to the whole conversation. Finally, she said, "Margie must have done something to Colleen. That is the only thing that makes sense."

"I could surmise that too honey," said Tom, "but trying to figure out what it is, or was, is beyond me."

"Well, we are all just going to have to think really hard as to what it could be. Certainly, Colleen could have cared less that Margie was rich. Colleen was never the envious type."

"I should put you on the stand to repeat what you just said." As the words came out of his mouth though, he knew his wife would never allow it. In fact, she visibly showed her disapproval by shaking her head no. Besides, neither would the prosecutor who would be constantly objecting.

They all sat around discussing the court proceedings that day while the parents enjoyed their cups of coffee. Finally, Tom said, "Just being around you guys makes me feel better. It's not that we solved anything unfortunately, but just discussing the generalities of the case with the three of you leaves me with a peace of mind I can't describe. At least now I'll be able to concentrate a little better when I go to my den to work... and who knows what I might find?" He gave them each a peck on the head as he excused himself from the table. The girls helped their mother clear the table, and while the mother went to do some seamstress work, the girls washed the dishes.

That evening when the parents were getting ready for bed and the girls were already asleep, Mrs. Wagner conveyed her fright to her husband. "I can't even begin to imagine what the O'Conner's are going through."

"Neither can I. That is the main reason I did not want to take this case. I am so close to the matter that there is not a minute that I don't put myself in the position of Jack and Doris."

"How do they do it honey? They both look so composed when I see them. You just never would know the horror they are experiencing."

"I've wondered about that myself. You sure can't tell by looking at them the hell they are enduring. I think having Jack's mother there does a lot for the whole family. She is a blessing in disguise. I don't think I could ever look like I have it all together."

"Well, that is the silliest thing I ever heard out of your mouth. Your composure as an attorney is to be admired. You never appear to look flustered or out of sorts. Perhaps your training has helped in that regard, but I do think your personality enhanced your position as a lawyer."

"Thanks Babe." Tom watched his wife strip down to her bra and garter belt. She sat on the edge of the bed to unhook her stockings and just the look of his wife doing that sent chills up Tom's spine. He walked over to her and sat beside her and unhooked her bra. Tom had no intention of letting this precious moment go to waste. At this instant, there were better things to do.

* * *

The mood at the Wagner's was much better the next morning. They all sat down to a breakfast of bacon, eggs, muffins and orange juice before proceeding to the courthouse.

Tom again was going to question Colleen before the court session. He really did not expect her responses to change – but he did have to try. Whatever Colleen was keeping secret, or withholding, depicted a loyalty he had never experienced, or could it be stubbornness he wondered. She would not tell even her parents, or her grandmother, let alone her friends. Tom could not imagine either of his girls reacting in this manner. Yet, it would be ludicrous not to attempt to get Colleen to release the information which Tom felt with certainty was vital to the case.

22

This was the second day of court. Tom was still in a daze as to how he could change the dismal scenario of the case. Girl after girl on the cheerleading squad almost had an agenda to convict Colleen. At least their testimony appeared that way. Yesterday, the prosecution made it clear that Colleen and Margie were having an argument, and by the time it got around to the last girl on the squad, one got the impression the fight had become violent and Colleen had never looked so angry. Tom kept objecting over and over, but the prosecution made their points to the jury each time another exaggeration was put forth.

Both the mothers of the deceased and of the person convicted, continued to wow the spectators with their outfits and their good looks. This was one case though where sheer beauty outweighed the extravagance of wealth. Margie's mother's face looked frozen in position as though not being able to show expression, the cause no doubt due to face lifts. Mrs. O'Conner on the other hand had this inner beauty that caused her to glow despite the horror she was experiencing. Both fathers were handsome in their own way. Margie's father had dark hair and a nice build, but something about him exuded almost a criminal appearance. Jack, on the other hand, had rugged good looks. The death of his father had taken a toll on his brown hair, so he was graying at the temples. He had a broad chest and wide shoulders and his suit only enhanced his appearance to make him appear more distinctive.

* * *

Roy and Rabbit were back in their own special place up in the upper far balcony of the courtroom. This area was usually set aside for the black population, or the negros as they were then called. Those without a lot of money also liked to squeeze themselves in that area sort of fearing that perhaps they did not even belong there, and those members of the population could be either Caucasian or of the Negro race. Roy's mother was almost glad the court proceedings were happening. It gave the two boys something productive to do with their lazy days that kept them occupied and out of trouble. Again, she made a nice lunch for both boys. When they would come home after the proceedings finished, she was happy to serve them milk and cookies while she sat and listened to them speak about everything that occurred that day in the courtroom.

Often, she looked at Rabbit, a pleasant enough child, and wondered what type of mother would just let their child roam the streets mooching off anyone he could. One thing for sure, Rabbit was always appreciative of any food he received, or if he ever spent the night, he always made sure to thank those who treated him well. Whether it was his mother, or someone else in his life, Rabbit was taught to be polite. Roy's mother did not spend a lot of time asking "why" though since she herself led a full, rich life and any child that came into her house was going to be fed, or otherwise, as long as the child treated her Roy appropriately and in a pleasant manner. The boys were becoming like two peas in a pod spending so much time together. The mother was not immune to feeling great sympathy for Colleen. She could not even imagine how she would react if her Roy were accused of something so horrible. Colleen was well liked in Roy's household, as were all in Colleen's family. Roy's dad often spent time at the bar, and the rest were used to seeing Colleen out and about the convenience store. As far as they were concerned, the law was accusing the wrong person of murder.

Once the bailiff called in Judge Stallone, the boys knew they had to sit and be quiet, but until that time, they peeked over the mahogany rail in the hope of seeing Colleen. Both boys swooned when they saw her.

This day was quite hot, and ladies got out their paper fans waving them back and forth to create a slight whiff of air while the men wiped their faces with white handkerchiefs. The electric fans had been blowing full blast all morning, but the humidity lived up to its name of being clammy, moist and damp. After an intense morning of questioning on both sides, and because of the heat and humidity, the session lasted until one o'clock in the afternoon and then the Judge dismissed everyone for the day.

The Chapman's were relieved there would be no court for the rest of the day. They immediately returned to their hotel and stripped out of their warm clothing. Mrs. Chapman took a bath while her husband took a shower. They desperately wanted to use the outdoor hotel pool but did not for fear of being approached by the journalists that seemed to be lurking around every nook and cranny. Instead, they ordered iced tea and lunch, and after it was brought to their room, they sat around in their underwear in the hope of getting cooler.

"So far, none of the girls have mentioned Margie's so-called sexual preferences."

"You can't get it in your head, how Margie really felt, can you babe."

"Margie talked nonsense. She was not a homosexual, and if she persisted in saying so, I had every intention of taking her out of the public school and sending her someplace where they could hopefully talk her out of it."

"It still can come up in court, and it is my understanding you can't talk someone out of their sexual preferences."

"What the hell do you know about it?"

"I looked it up in our Encyclopedia Britannica."

"Britannica, dumbannica! Such nonsense."

"Well, it said there are four possibilities of why homosexuality could happen to an individual. It could be an endocrine disorder, a genetic aberration, a psychological condition, or a mixture of two or more of these. Females are called lesbians. This behavior can also be found in animals."

"Oh, for crying out loud, stop talking such nonsense. Where does the encyclopedia gets its information for them to act like an authority anyway?"

"I notice you use the encyclopedia often enough when you have a question where we don't know the answer."

"That is on a legitimate topic."

"This is legitimate. You just don't want to accept it. The ancient Greeks considered homosexual behavior normal. Consequences of the death penalty in our own country has failed to stamp it out."

"My God, you are now acting like an authority on the subject, just because you read that stupid encyclopedia."

"I'm just trying to understand my daughter, and I'm far from being an authority. Sigmund Freud first developed the idea of psychological causation believing that males become too attached to their mothers and are hostile to their fathers. So, males adopt their mother's feminine mannerisms. I don't know if I agree with everything I've read, but it never hurts to become more educated about anything."

"Sigmund Freud is a jerk too as far as I am concerned."

"Obviously, you have no interest on the topic, and since our daughter is no longer alive, I certainly am not going to try and make you understand. Frankly, even after looking it up, I'm still not sure I understand. Hopefully, in years to come, either they will comprehend the topic better, or maybe we won't have to be concerned any longer. Just don't be shocked if it is still brought up in the courtroom."

"If it is, I will be so embarrassed I can't predict my reactions."

"Great, you have now given me something else about which to be concerned."

The heat, the conversation, and the day in court got the best of the Chapmans. They both decided to take a much-needed nap. When they awoke and had room service bring in their dinner, they dressed casually and decided to drive by their old home. They asked the gal who brought their dinner if she knew of a discreet exit for the hotel where they would not be noticed and if they could also park their car there when they returned that evening. The waitress did know, and that is the exit they used for the rest of the trial to avoid the myriad of news reporters and journalists.

23

During the weekend, severe thunderstorms pounded the area with even some hail noticed in a few of the neighborhoods. People were happy to be inside their homes or hotel rooms since no court sessions were scheduled during the weekend. When Monday morning rolled around, the temperatures in the area had cooled quite a bit. It was a welcome relief to everyone that was expected in court that day as well as the spectators that would not miss the goings on for anything.

Some of Doris's friends visited her on Saturday and Sunday and brought her some of their best clothes to try on so she would not have to repeat wearing any item of clothing while her daughter was being tried. They wanted their friend to look every bit as good as those city people. Today Doris was going to wear a slim beige skirt and lighter beige blouse with short sleeves and a black collar. With it she wore a black three-inch wide leather belt with a fashionable large gold buckle. The belt accented Doris' tiny waist. If the electric fans were kept blowing in court, despite the cooler temperatures, Doris brought a black cardigan sweater to wear. The outfit was topped off with black shoes that had a narrow four-inch heel. Around her neck she wore a gold cross and chain. A crucifix of Jesus was attached to the cross. As she left her bedroom to go downstairs, she momentarily grabbed the cross in her hand while it was on her neck. She kept her folded hand against her chest as she looked up to the heavens. She said a quick prayer before venturing down the steps.

"The coffee smells good Ma." It took Doris a while to get used to calling her mother-in-law either Ma or Mom, but she soon began to realize that

Cora was indeed the best mother anyone could want. At her place at the table was a half grapefruit already cut in sections that Doris quickly devoured. No sooner had she finished, when two sunny side up eggs were placed before her with buttered toast and jelly. Jack had already eaten and was tending to some paperwork for the convenience store and bar before they ventured on over to the courthouse. They were attempting to do anything that would distract themselves from a situation that appeared gloomier every day.

"Why don't you finish getting ready to go to court, Ma? I'll straighten up in the kitchen, and thanks for a super breakfast."

"Oh no, dear. It's such a lovely day, I decided to walk to the courthouse today. I don't need to be at court as early as the two of you, and if I do get tired, there is always somebody I know who is willing to give me a lift."

"This is an exciting day, Ma. The prosecution completed their testimonies yesterday, and today Mr. Wagner is going to have his day in court."

"I know, I would not miss it for anything. Also, he may call Mia and Barbara to the stand."

"Well, he already stressed to us that calling them to testify is not going to bring about anything new. So far, Colleen's case is looking very weak, and I'm very concerned."

"I know dear. I guess at this point we just have to have faith in our dear Lord."

Jack walked into the kitchen and said to his wife, "Wow, you look terrific honey. Everyone in court is going to have their eyes on you. You'll be just the distraction I need, because to be honest, I am worried sick."

"I know, hon. I feel so inwardly sad, but thank you for the kind compliment."

"It's not kind Doris. You are a knockout every day but today especially so. I think we had better get going. Where's Ma, isn't she going to court today?"

"She is. I think she brought the trash out to the back porch. However, she is not coming with us. She wants to walk over to court today."

"Oh ok. I'll find her to tell her we are leaving. You can get in the car."

* * *

The weekend appeared to invigorate the crowd in the courtroom, while the weather also seemed to revitalize the spectators. The noise level had reached such an upsurge it was almost a relief when the bailiff announced Judge Stallone would be entering at that point. This caused the noise to diminish greatly.

Despite the jail attire, Colleen managed to look good every day which was sort of a shock to people who expected otherwise. Her grandmother had brought Colleen her own personal hairbrush which softened the red curls around Colleen's face helping her to have an angelic look. The only thing still lacking was the smile one usually saw on Colleen's beautiful face. The face everyone in court saw had no expression whatsoever.

It was hard to figure exactly what Colleen was thinking. Her thoughts never strayed far from the incident in the girls' room. Colleen went over and over in her head what had occurred that particular day. Did I indicate to Margie that I felt more about her than just the normal friendship I have with Barbara and Mia. What was it I did? This was typical of Colleen, to blame herself. No matter the scenario, it always came back to blaming herself. Were my actions flirtatious? I did not even know Margie was going to be in the girls' room for heaven's sake. Also, I never completed what I really went in there to do. All three of us were always nice to Margie. What made her do that to just me? Of course, I'll never know what she did to the other girls either since they might keep it a secret too. Why me Margie? And, who killed you?

Barbara got up to testify. Every time she attempted to say what a wonderful friend and person Colleen was, the prosecutor objected claiming relevance, and most of the time Judge Stallone agreed that what was being said had no place in the proceedings. Mr. Wagner felt more despondent when they recessed for lunch. He literally had nothing to prove Colleen's innocence unless they could pinpoint the time of death and when the young man had walked her home.

Roy and Rabbit did not leave for lunch until the courtroom was practically empty. They leaned over the railing to watch everyone and the normal commotion that ensued. Mostly, they waited until Colleen was taken from the room. They then ran and grabbed their bikes and went back to the wooded area behind the school where Margie's body was found.

"Why did we come here? This area gives me the creeps," said Rabbit.

"It might be creepy now because of the murder, but this was one of our favorite places to play before everything happened. Besides, I'm just trying to figure what happened that day. First of all, it's not like Colleen ever got in a fight with anyone. It just doesn't make sense either that Colleen would attack someone from behind."

"What makes you say that?"

"The Coroner said Margie was hit strongly on the back of the head."

24

After eating another great lunch and playing by the creek that also ran behind the school's wooded area, the boys packed up their belongings and proceeded to leave. It was at that moment that Rabbit started acting very strange.

"What's up Buddy?" This was the term of expression they called each other when they knew something was wrong.

Rabbit didn't answer. His body was doubled over and he held his head in his hands.

"Look, if you are sick, I need to go and get someone."

That seemed to grab Rabbit's attention. His body straightened, and he almost shouted, "No, don't get anybody."

Remembering what his mother did, Roy ran to the nearby creek and dampened a napkin his mother had included in the lunches. He ran back, told Rabbit to lie down on a patch of leaves and pressed the damp cloth against Rabbit's forehead. He also put a jacket as a sort of a pillow under the back of his neck. Whether it was a logical thing to do, or not, Rabbit's state of mind appeared to be somewhat better.

At this point, Roy realized they would not make it back to court on time, but the situation with his friend prioritized not even thinking about returning to court that day.

Rabbit attempted to talk, but the words just would not come out of his mouth.

"You sure you don't want me to go get a doctor or someone who can help?"

"Yea, I'm sure."

At that statement, Roy just sat on the ground beside his friend. When it appeared they were going to be there forever, Roy finally said, "Either you tell me what is wrong, or I will leave you here and go for help. You no longer have a choice in the matter."

For a moment it looked like Roy was going to have to go for help. Then, out of nowhere, Rabbit said, "I was here in the woods that day with Margie."

"What? Are you saying you saw Colleen kill Margie? Oh my God!"

"No, no. I did not say that at all."

"Well, what did you say Rabbit. What?"

"It was the day you had to find out something for your mother with the Principal, and you had to wait for the Principal to finish with someone else."

"Yea, so what?"

"I was trying to think of something to do until you finished."

"Ok, so what did you do?"

"I went to the woods in back of the school...in back of the girls' room."

"So, you go there a lot. You told me nobody bothers you there, and you would wait there that day until I came and got you."

"That's right. It's peaceful back here. I like to sit near the creek and watch the water running and sometimes cup my hands and take a drink. The water is always so cool and fresh."

"What's that got to do with Margie anyhow?" Rabbit started to cry uncontrollably.

"Oh, Rabbit, it's ok if you saw the two girls fighting. Don't cry."

"You don't understand. I didn't see the two girls." The tears came faster.

"Quit kidding around with me. We've already missed this afternoon's session in court because of the strange way you are acting."

All of a sudden, Rabbit realized he could not say more. His crying stopped and he said to Roy, "I just want to go home. I've told you too much already."

"Told me too much? Are you crazy? You haven't told me a darn thing. And, when I did come and get you that day, there was no yellow police tape around. Though, come to think of it, you were not your normal self. We are not going home until you tell me what you saw."

The tears started all over again. Rabbit sat on the ground and leaning over folded his arms around his head which he put in his lap.

"You are driving me crazy. I am your Buddy. We tell each other everything, so I am not leaving here until you tell me why you are crying, and neither are you."

"You've got to promise me you won't tell anyone else."

"Oh, for crying out loud. Who am I going to tell?"

"Promise me?"

"Yea, I promise you. Now tell me."

"I was by the creek when I heard someone mumbling. I turned around, and I saw Margie. I was trying to see if she was talking to someone before I went up to her, but I did not see anyone."

"What was she saying."

"It sounded to me like she kept repeating herself, over and over. The sounds I heard sounded like What made me think Colleen was interested in me. Why did I make advances toward her? However, it all sounded so silly that I thought I must not have heard her correctly."

"So?"

"Anyway, she just kept walking around in circles mumbling the same thing. At least it sounded that way. It was then I thought I would go to her and see if I could help."

Roy looked at Rabbit expecting him to elaborate some more. "I turned around to get my books by the creek, and when I looked in the direction where I had seen her, she was no longer there. The woods can get pretty dense, so I was not surprised I could not see her then, but I kept looking."

This story was going on forever, but Roy knew that if he nudged Rabbit in any way, he might make things worse, so he waited for more.

"I could hear the mumbling again, so I followed the noise." A sweat broke out on Rabbit's face. "Actually, I was hoping that by then you were finished with the Principal and we could both approach her together. I always felt a little strange around Margie." Rabbit noticed Roy getting restless. "I'm almost finished."

"Good – continue."

"The noise got really loud, but at this point it was like she was speaking in tongues or something, and I still couldn't see her. We both went around that tall bush a different direction and we ran into each other. Scared the you know what right out of me."

"Ok, so you were both scared."

At this point the tears were back in Rabbit's eyes.

"Now what?"

"She got so scared she tripped on a twig causing her to fall backward." Rabbit walked to a huge rock where Margie fell and pointed to it. She collapsed so fast I didn't have time to grab her. She hit the back of her head, and she didn't move. I got so scared; I ran right away 'cause I knew nobody would ever believe Rabbit."

Roy stood there in a daze not saying anything while trying to comprehend what he had just heard.

"That's why you nearly ran into me that day running so fast when I came out of the Principal's office? Though, you did slow down once you saw me and we walked on home. Why didn't you say anything at that time?"

"You are kidding right? Who is going to believe a negro boy? Especially one with a strange background. You can already see how everyone is calling it a murder."

"That's only because Margie's death was so strange. What a horrible way to die."

"Yea, well, it's true, and I had nothing to do with it, so I got outta there fast."

"My God though Rabbit, our Colleen is being accused of killing her. Those girls on the cheerleading squad are convinced she did it, and they in turn are swaying the minds of the jurors. She may be put in jail for a long, long time for something she didn't do."

"A jury would never convict a pretty white girl like Colleen. It is better this way."

25

Roy was completely in disbelief at what he was hearing and said to Rabbit, "Wow, what a distorted way of thinking."

"Well, you wouldn't think so if you was my color."

"Do you really believe that Rabbit?"

"I ain't stupid!"

"Let's go back and sit down by the creek. We have to decide what we are going to do."

"I ain't going back in that woods ever again. Anyway, there is nothing to do 'cause you promised me you would not tell anyone. So, there!"

They walked out of the woods and away from the school, pushing their bikes beside them with their hands. Roy was speechless for a long time. They passed the town soda shop and could hear people talking about the case. Apparently, court was still in session, and running later than what was normal.

"Here, hold my bike," Roy requested of Rabbit. "I'll go in and buy us both an ice cream cone. What flavor do you want, and do you want a sugar cone or cake cone?"

"Get me black cherry on a cake cone and thank you." When Roy came out, he had Rabbit's request and a sugar cone for himself topped with chocolate ice cream. They steered their bikes over to the adjacent park and sat on a bench in a quiet area.

They ate slowly savoring each bite and licking the sides of the cone where the ice cream was quickly melting. Roy handed Rabbit his handkerchief to clean his hands before Rabbit handed it back and Roy cleaned his own hands. Each one sat there deep in their own thoughts.

"We've got to tell Mr. Wagner, Rabbit, or somebody. We just do."

"Uh, uh. No, we don't and YOU promised."

Roy sighed. "Buddy, this is the first time in my life I am doing this, but I have to break my promise to you. It was an accident, plain and simple. They can't possibly charge you."

"NO, you can't do that. You promised, and besides, how you going to prove that?"

Gosh, thought Roy. Maybe Rabbit is right. It's just two silly boys with no proof whatsoever – one boy is Caucasian and the other one Negro. That makes for an even odder situation because mixed races aren't supposed to associate with one another. "Should we tell my Ma Rabbit? Maybe she can think of something that we can't."

"NO!"

Some people (probably visitors to the court from out of town because the boys didn't recognize them) were walking by and turned around when Rabbit shouted out and looked the boys over with a strangeness that was hard to detect.

"Keep your voice down Rabbit. We must come up with a plan. Do you have any ideas?"

"I told you my idea. To just shut up about the whole darn thing."

"That's not an option Rabbit, and you know it."

"It'd better be. Don't make me sorry I told ya."

"What if the jury does decide to convict our pretty white friend? What then? She's always been as nice as she could be to you and me. She doesn't care what color we are, cares nothing about our upbringing, nor how much money anybody has or doesn't have. Would you honestly stay quiet if they convicted her of the so-called crime?"

Rabbit didn't answer. Instead he got up from the bench and started walking back and forth, back and forth. Eventually, he did sit down again, but nothing came out of his mouth. It was getting near supper time.

"I've got to get on home Rabbit. We've been gone all afternoon. Ma may think we are just now getting out of court, but someone is sure to tell her we never went back after lunch time. We'd better come up with something to tell her before she asks."

"Just tell her it was such a nice day we decided not to go back to court but stayed out in the fresh air instead."

"She's going to miss our daily update from the courtroom."

Again, Rabbit snapped back his answer when he said, "Well, today she's just going to have to miss it – that's all there is to it."

"You know Rabbit? I don't even like you right now. Just find someplace else to go. I'm going home alone."

Rabbit looked at Roy with shock. "What – are you going to tattle-tale everything to your Ma?"

"Not right now, but if you continue to treat me like a piece of shit, I just may decide to do so."

Hearing the swear word come out of Roy's mouth was a bit of a shock. He was not the kind of person to just throw swear words here and there except in an unusual situation. Oddly, though, Rabbit could not seem to comprehend this was an unusual situation.

"Well, what am I going to do?"

"I don't know, you'll figure it out. You always do," said Roy.

* * *

Roy never felt in such a dilemma in his entire life. What was he going to do? He parked his bike in the backyard shed and went in the house through the kitchen door. The screen door made a loud bang. The smell of spaghetti sauce filled his nostrils, and he immediately felt better. To Roy, good old spaghetti and meatballs was feel-good food. His mother could not have chosen a better menu if she had planned it that way.

"Is that you honey?" Roy could hear his mother's pleasing voice coming from the living room. "I'm knitting in the living room."

Just as she said that, Roy walked in the room. He went over to his Mom and kissed her on the forehead. "That sauce smells delicious. I almost can't wait for dinner."

"I made a big pot to satisfy not only your Dad and me, but there's plenty extra for you and Rabbit too. Where is Rabbit by the way?" She said this as she peeked behind Roy to see if Rabbit were following him.

"He did not come back with me. He won't be having dinner here tonight."

"Why not? What on earth is he going to do?"

"I'm not sure. He didn't say." All of what he was saying was true, yet Roy felt like a liar somehow.

"How did it go in court today?"

"We only went this morning, and when they broke for lunch it was so nice out that we never went back. I did buy us some ice cream though."

Oddly, that statement seemed to pacify his mother as she said, "It was a beautiful day today. I guess I can understand two healthy boys not wanting to be cooped up inside all day. Also, good for you for giving a treat to Rabbit and for yourself. Nothing like ice cream on a nice summer day."

His Dad came home from the factory and put his lunch pail on the table. Having also entered through the kitchen, his wife heard the screen door slam a second time. She put her knitting aside on her way to see her husband who gave her a good kiss on the lips and patted Roy on the head.

"Smells great in here," said the father.

"I'll ask Roy to help me set the table while you go up and take your shower."

Roy grabbed his father's lunch pail, opened it up and cleaned it out. While washing the thermos, Roy said, "Dad must have liked what you made him for lunch Ma. Everything is gone."

"Great! That's what I like to hear."

26

That evening, Roy had a restless sleep. His mother and father took turns going to his room every time he yelled out. One time his mother found he had broken out in a sweat so severely that his head looked like he had run under a hose. She gently got a towel and patted him dry while also removing his white armless t-shirt. She never bothered to put a new top on him, and oddly, he slept through the whole process.

She thought her son was getting terribly ill and discussed the matter while in bed with her husband. "No honey, I just think the court proceedings are upsetting Roy. Afterall, he always did have a crush on Colleen, and I've heard rumors that things are not looking in her favor. Maybe we should forbid him from going to court."

"I'm not so sure that we could forbid him without a fight. I'll give it some thought though if you really think it will help. In fact, I'll be concerned about it all night, as there is no way I am going to sleep now."

Sirens could be heard in the distance and then they appeared to be rather close. In fact, Roy could see the vehicles coming down the road, their sirens getting louder and louder and the headlights were brighter showing through Roy's bedroom window with the red flashing lights creating strange images on the walls of his room. Just as one car stopped in front of Roy's house, the sirens stopped, and Roy woke up screaming. His whimpering already had brought both parents to his room and this blood curdling scream came out of Roy's mouth as soon as his mother turned on the overhead light.

"Roy, Roy, wake up honey. What's wrong?"

"The police are coming to get me. Check outside Ma."

"No one is outside honey; you are having a nightmare." The mother engulfed the child in her arms to try and comfort him.

Roy started shaking uncontrollably. His father finally said, "Why would the police be after you Roy? Did you do something wrong?"

"No, I ah…I just know something."

"Well, tell us what it is."

"I can't. I promised I wouldn't tell anyone."

The mother and father glanced at each other. There were so many different ways they could handle this questioning. They wanted to be sure to do the right thing.

"You promised who?"

"I can't tell you."

"Maybe, for once you NEED to tell us."

"You always told me Ma that when someone trusted you with a promise, you should never reveal that promise."

"Unless the promise gives you nightmares. You just can't keep acting irrationally. Does this have anything to do with Colleen?"

Roy didn't answer.

"I guess the three of us can sit here all night until you decide to talk."

Then the mother said, "I have a good feeling that this has something to do with Rabbit. That's probably why he didn't come for supper tonight."

Roy looked up at his mother as she said that, and he was amazed at her motherly intuition. Still, he said nothing.

The father spoke then with such a sternness that Roy knew he was not going to get away with this charade much longer. The guilt he began to feel at possibly betraying his friend almost caused him to again break out in a sweat.

For something to do in the awkward silence, Roy's mother went over to the bedside lamp and turned it on. Then she shut off the overhead light thinking if the lighting were more subdued that additional information could be more forthcoming. It might be easier to speak if one were not so visible to others. It seemed to work.

Sitting on the bed beside Roy, she said, "Please dear, tell us what is wrong. We are only here to help you and not to judge either you or Rabbit." However, as she said that a horrible fear clutched her mind, and it was felt in her stomach. My God, what if one of these two boys is actually Margie's murderer? No, it can't be. As obnoxious as they can both be sometimes, there is nothing in their personalities to imply they could murder anyone.

Roy thought a lot about what he was about to do. In his heart he felt that there was no way the law would convict Rabbit. In reality, he was not so sure after listening to Rabbit's explanation of the circumstances. The accident, to Roy, was obvious. However, how society would accept the coincidental fact of both Margie and Rabbit being in the same woods at the same time seemed highly improbable. And, of course, one was female, one a male, and one was Caucasian and the other Negro. He did know though that if anyone could help it would be his parents. The bottom line was he had to break his promise to his friend, and that was the hardest part of all.

"It was all an accident. Nobody murdered Margie."

"Ok, how do you know that?"

"Rabbit told me."

"Telling you something doesn't mean it is right."

"I know that, but it was the concern on his face and his reaction in the woods when he told me."

"You went back to the woods behind the school?"

"Yea, Ma. You know that's our favorite place to play. Also, it wasn't as far from the courthouse as the place near the lake where we had gone before."

"What made Rabbit tell you?"

"He started breaking out in a sweat, and he wasn't going to tell me. When I said his condition meant I needed to go get someone, he almost became belligerent. Then he gave in a little. I had to promise not to tell anyone though."

"Honey, your words are always important," the father said. "Also, to have someone trust you to not defy them is equally so. Yet, the promises always must be made in consideration of someone else should that problem ever arise. If it means by keeping a promise someone else might be hurt, then it takes a bigger person to give that consideration and perhaps reveal what has been told."

Roy thought about what his father said a lot. His father was not a man of many words, so when he said something, it was inevitable that it was important and required scrutiny. If Colleen were convicted that would be intolerable. On the other hand, if she were set free, no harm would be done. Oh, the dilemma. Yet, Margie's parents have a right to know how she died. For them to always think that someone murdered their pride and joy had to create many concerns for the unfortunate parents. Roy guessed he was going to have to finish his tale.

It was about four in the morning when everyone calmed down and Roy had finished telling his story. The parents told him they were all going to sleep on the message and try to figure out what to do the next day.

Once Roy had that load off his chest, he had no problem falling back to sleep. One thing in his favor was that it was summer, and he did not have to awaken early for school. He had no plans to go sit in the courtroom the next day either. His parents had more difficulty falling back to sleep, but slumber eventually overcame them both. Roy's father had already made up his mind he was not going to work the next day. He and his wife had to figure out what must be done about this whole horrible situation.

* * *

The Mom made a hearty breakfast of pancakes with maple syrup and lots of sausages. She had canned peaches earlier in the year, along with other food, and a Mason jar of the fruit had been brought up from the basement.'

Sugar was still hard to get as it was one of the items that was rationed because of the war, so they learned to drink their coffee black. The fact made her happy though that she had picked up her canning sugar early in the season. All people had rationing stamps for sugar, but those who canned got extra stamps for canning sugar. However, just because you had stamps was no guarantee you would get the sugar because shipment of the sugar was still scarce. Whether it was knowledge of this fact, or not, the peaches seemed to taste extra good that day.

During the early morning before Mr. Wagner left his home, Roy's mother called him stating she had extremely important information relevant to the murder case. Hearing that, Mr. Wagner asked Roy's parents to meet him in his office at 8 o'clock that morning. It did not give them much time since the court proceedings started at ten in the morning. Roy was to spend the day with his grandmother who lived at the other end of town. The grandmother came to get Roy. Eventually he would have to talk, but not today.

27

Mr. Wagner's assistant immediately brought Roy's parents back to Mr. Wagner's office as soon as they arrived. He offered them both a seat and inquired if they wanted some coffee before starting. They both declined the offer for coffee.

"How may I help you today? We'll have to make this quick since I have to be in court by 10 or preferably a little earlier than that."

The mother spoke first stating, "I really don't know where to start except to say Colleen didn't kill Margie, it was an accident."

Mr. Wagner's look was one of sheer astonishment. "What makes you say that?"

Roy's father took over the conversation when he said, "You know Rabbit, is that right Mr. Wagner?" It appeared that everyone knew Rabbit as Tom shook his head yes. "Rabbit, was waiting for Roy in the woods that day that Margie died. He saw it happen."

Tom was not so sure. "If that is true, why didn't Rabbit come forth sooner? In fact, I've seen him and Roy in court a lot. He should have said something, or your son should have."

"Our son just found out yesterday, and he's been up all night with nightmares. He had promised Rabbit he would not say anything concerning what Rabbit told him before Rabbit revealed the story to him. Rabbit did not come forward because of the fact that he's colored. He felt no one would believe him."

At first, Tom poo pooed the idea thinking it all was a lot of nonsense. Then, having represented many coloreds in his practice he began to appreciate the quandary Rabbit faced. He understood that Rabbit was correct in his thinking that people would think him the guilty one because of his race. "Does he have any proof that it was an accident?"

"Not really, except he always waited in the wooded area for Roy who that day had an appointment with the school Principal. He said that usually there were not a lot of kids in that area right after school, so he felt more comfortable waiting there than waiting in the front of school where often he was the victim of abuse and name calling by the other students."

"Well, unfortunately, we cannot just take the boys at their word. We must find out if this is true. More investigation will be forthcoming and eventually Roy and Rabbit will have to be questioned by me, and the prosecution and Judge will be involved."

"That will only happen if we can be present when the two boys are questioned."

"What about Rabbit's parents? Are they in the picture?"

"We have no information about them except to say I don't believe there is a responsible father, and often we feed Rabbit and provide him a place to sleep. Other times, we don't know where he sleeps, and he and Roy got in a fight yesterday, so we have no idea where he is presently." The mother looked distraught. Her only intention was to help her son Roy and stand up for Rabbit, but she had the feeling they were just making things worse."

"What you just told me will not bode well with the court. Where is Roy now?"

"He did not sleep well at all last night and had several nightmares. His grandmother has him at her home for the day."

"Ok, I'm going to go over to the courthouse and ask the judge to call off the proceedings at least for today. Why don't you both come with me. I think having you present will help to bring more credence to what must be said."

Both husband and wife agreed.

It was about 9:30 a.m. when Mr. Wagner asked if they could speak to Judge Stallone. The prosecutor was also notified, and they all went to the Judge's chambers. "Let's get right to the point here as the trial continues at 10 a.m."

"Your honor, we have reason to believe that Margaret Chapman was not murdered, but she got hurt accidentally. You know of Roy and Rabbit as do most people in this town. These are Roy's parents." He pointed to Roy's mother and father who were asked by the Judge why they thought Margie was not murdered.

The prosecutor expressed grave doubts about what he had just heard, and even the Judge looked skeptical. However, the Judge looked at the no nonsense parents and decided the situation required some attention. Finally, at 10 minutes to 10 o'clock, the Judge said he would stop the court proceedings temporarily to investigate if what Roy and Rabbit said could possibly be true.

At ten o'clock on the button, Judge Stallone entered the courtroom, and everyone rose from their seats at the bailiff's instructions. Sitting on the Bench, Judge Stallone eyed the packed courtroom. He mentally told himself he was about to shock everyone there when he finally said, "There will be no court in session today. A matter has come up that requires our attention. The court may possibly open tomorrow. I have no guarantee of that though at this time." The Jury was instructed not to read any newspapers or listen to the news. Neither were they to speak to family members, or others, about the case. "You will be notified as to when we should return to court."

An odd rumble swept the courtroom area along with audible gasps as everyone appeared to be in shock. Of course, speculation outdid itself and rumors were flying all over the place. Journalists were attempting to discover any little tidbit they could find to print without a lot of success.

The O'Conners and the Chapmans sat in their seats not sure what they should do. Both attorneys thought that the less said the better. They did not want to give either of the parents any false hope. In Colleen's case, it could possibly mean a drop in the charges and freedom once again. In Margie's case, the parents still would have the loss of their daughter, but some of the sting might possibly be removed if they knew no one had murdered her.

However, their attorneys tactfully avoided the real reason and paraphrasing, both men as much as said that something came up that could possibly altar the case. Examination of the new assertions had to be investigated before going further.

Not only were the journalists baffled, but the parents too had more speculation to endure.

28

Back at the hotel, the Chapmans were beside themselves.

"What could it be that is causing this delay? I don't need any of this. I want it to end now." The wife was acting very dramatically.

"I'm affected by this too as much as you are, so stop being so theatrical."

"This is the way I personally feel. It has nothing to do with dramatics."

"You couldn't prove it by me."

"Gosh, why are we fighting over this anyway. Things are tough enough without us getting into a fight.

"You're right babe, I'm sorry. You should remember though that this is also affecting me. Your actions don't always show it."

"I know, maybe I was being a little dramatic, and if so, I apologize."

* * *

At the O'Conner's house the court delay was also the topic of conversation. Only, they were more concerned about their daughter's state of mind than their own.

"Each day this spectacle is delayed has to be hard on our daughter," said Doris.

"I know honey, I can't imagine what she is going through right now."

"We'll go over to the dungeon and talk to her later. Doris always called the jail a dungeon. I was stunned when they brought her back to that place. Frankly, I was so concerned about what the Judge had just said, but it really bothered me when I saw them take her back to jail. I had hoped we would have a chance to talk to her, yet I instinctively knew they would not let us talk to her at that time anyway."

The Grandmother just sat quietly listening to all they had to say. She was in the courtroom when the Judge made his statement and was as shocked as everyone else. A wise woman, she knew sometimes you shouldn't speak unless someone spoke to you. She had her concerns as much as anyone but knew it would serve no purpose to presently voice them. In a little while, Jack would go check things at the bar, and she would let Doris vent her frustrations when he did.

Once Jack left the room, it was Doris that asked her mother-in-law if she wanted to accompany her to see Colleen. "I figure since they weren't planning on her being there at this time of day, it might be a good time to go there."

"That's a great idea. Of course, I'll go." They finished doing some routine things around the house, and since it was such a nice day, they both walked to get some fresh air.

Mr. Wagner was just leaving the facility when they both arrived. "What's going on?" Doris said this soon after greeting Tom.

"I'm not at liberty to say. The Judge thought it wise to wait and see if whatever information we received pans out after it gets investigated. All I will say, and it was just what I told Colleen, is if we can prove some things, it will be to her benefit. Just support her now, and I hope you don't ask her a lot of questions because she really doesn't know any more than you or I do."

Disappointment filled Doris' face, but she graciously shook Tom's hand and promised to do as he said.

Colleen was happy to see her mother and grandmother. The first question out of her mouth though was, "Why didn't we have court today? What's happening?"

"I'm not quite sure what's happening, honey. Since we were not going to be near you in court today, we decided that the best thing to do would be to come and see you here. I guess these things happen, and we're just going to have to put our trust in the system."

"That sounds good Mom, like you have been trained to say it. The thing is, I have manufactured a schedule in my head to see how much I could endure before the trial ended. Now, this delay screws up everything."

"Sorry, Colleen." Thinking it better to attempt to change the subject the mother asked, "Is there anything we can get you that you might possibly need?"

Before answering, Colleen acknowledged her grandmother and apologized for not doing so sooner. The atmosphere became more social after Doris changed the subject, and the visit turned out to be better than had been anticipated.

"I notice Roy and Rabbit in the upper section and caught them smiling at me one time. However, they did not return one afternoon, and I did not see them this morning in court. Is either one of them sick?"

"Hmm, oh, wow, I'm not sure darling. I haven't noticed either one to be honest with you."

Colleen thought her mother's demeanor odd, but nothing anymore was as it used to be. "Where's Dad?"

"Since we have the day off, he thought he would check things at the bar, and he was going to work and help them out. He figured the bar would be busy today since the court was not in session."

"He's probably right. Funny how when the people take the day off from work and then find out things have changed, none of them choose to go back to work that day. I can't even imagine taking a day off from work to go to court. Why are people so interested, anyway?"

Both women decided not to answer Colleen. They could imagine a multitude of reasons why people wanted to be there. Not all of them were good either.

Virtuous at her distraction skills, Cora had written down all the names of the people who had asked about Colleen. "These are the names, sweetheart, of all the people who are concerned, and they ask me always how you are doing? The list of people was getting so long, I thought it would be best to write down all their names for you."

"Thanks, Grandma. How thoughtful of you. I hate it here and can't wait to come home."

"I know, honey. Up to now I've been admiring how well you have adjusted to this place and to everything that has happened. Please, don't give up now."

The two women decided to leave. Tears came to their eyes as they blew kisses to the beautiful child and whispered a prayer this would all end soon. Saying goodbye was always the hardest thing to do. They learned that being quick was the best approach and left Colleen with some reading material as they departed. Every time they entered the jail, all the items anyone brought for Colleen had to be checked by security.

29

All the new evidence was investigated, and Roy was brought to the Judge along with his parents to tell what he knew. Rabbit was nowhere to be found, even after questioning his mother who pretty much did not appear concerned about his whereabouts.

"Why didn't Rabbit come forward and tell us what he knew?" The Judge asked the question.

"Sir, Rabbit is a negro, and Margie was white. He feared no one would believe what he had to say. They would probably accuse him of the crime. He was scared and didn't tell me until the other day," Roy interjected.

"Do you realize Roy that witnesses are not supposed to attend the trial?"

"No Sir, I didn't know that, but I didn't commit any crime Sir, and I was not there when it happened. So, I couldn't be a witness anyway. I had an appointment with the Principal the day Margie died. The Principal's records should show that, and Rabbit always waited for me there in the woods because when he waited in the front of the school, the other students hanging around were nasty to him."

"But you say Rabbit was there in court with you?"

"What he did was not my fault."

"Of course, you are right, and I thank you for coming forward now."

The court delay lasted more than a week. The delay was hard on Colleen and her family.

Investigators went back to the school to question the Janitor after hearing through the grape vine that he had seen Colleen leave the girls' room.

"Why didn't you come forward with the information you are now telling us."

"Nobody asked me to."

"You could have come forward on your own accord."

"Why would I do that? I have a family sir. I'm not out looking for trouble."

Frustration on the faces of the investigators was quite obvious.

"Do you realize that by not telling us what you know, a sweet innocent girl might spend the rest of her life in jail, or even be put to death?"

"The Court, nor the Jury, is going to let that sweet white girl go to jail. No way!"

"Why do you say that?"

"If I came and told you what I saw, you would twist it to make me, a black man, look guilty. Not so for sweet Miss Colleen. I ain't stupid. I'm black and she's white, and you can count on that. No white person is going to put another white person to death in this small town. I ain't dumb either."

"What exactly did you see?"

"I was carrying some trash out to the cans in the back of the school. When I passed the girls' room, Colleen was leaving the room and she turned to go back in the school. She's always nice to me, but this day I noticed she looked sad, and she didn't say hello to me. There were other people in the hallway who had to see her too. Right behind her came Miss Margie who walked out the back entrance of the school towards the woods. I put up the signs saying do not enter and went in the girls' room to empty the trash. When I went out back to put the trash in the cans, I could hear a noise in the woods. I looked up and Miss Margie was walking around agitated in circles. She kept mumbling lots of words. Next thing I know, Rabbit comes around a bush and he and Miss Margie scared one another. She stepped back and tripped over something and fell backward. After that, I went back in the school figgering Rabbit would take care of her. Of course, I had no way of knowing how bad her fall was at that time until I later heard she died."

* * *

Rabbit had gone to the neighboring town to stay with a friend he met when the two rival towns played football together. It was a rivalry that had gone on for many years. "I hear they are looking for you Rabbit," said his friend after Rabbit had been with him a couple of days.

"Whose lookin for me?"

"The police."

"I knew Roy couldn't keep a secret."

"What secret?"

"Just sumpin between him and me."

"Now you know the police don't go looking for just anybody. You must know some important information. What's the secret you told Roy?"

"I ain't going to tell anymore people. Just get me in trouble."

"Maybe Roy didn't tell anybody. Think about that!"

"I'm in trouble, and I didn't do anything."

"Do you think that pretty girl murdered the other girl?"

Without thinking, Rabbit said, "I knows she didn't."

"Oh, how in the hell do you know that?"

Rabbit's hand went immediately to his mouth as though he could still shut it, even though he let out a big gasp.

"Now, you sees what you made me do?" The more nervous Rabbit got, his English became worse.

"Rabbit, if the police are looking for you, they will find you. You should go to them first. It might help your situation, whatever it is."

All Rabbit could do was bite his fingernails to the brim. One started to bleed, and this created a lot of commotion. His friend took him by the hand while saying, "Let my Mom take care of you and then we are all going to the police station."

"No, I ain't going to no police."

"Yes, you are, or we will all be in trouble."

"Why you goin to be in trouble?"

"We will be accused of hiding you."

Rabbit kept reneging and just sat there quietly as the Mom washed and took care of his finger. While she worked, his friend told his mother everything that he knew and followed it up by suggesting to her that they should drive Rabbit to the police station. As soon as the mother finished, Rabbit attempted to make a quick escape, but the mother grabbed him by the arm and harshly told him to sit down in the chair. She instructed her son to get her purse and car keys off the hallway table. Mom and son each grabbed an arm, and they told Rabbit to get up and come with them to the car. She instructed Rabbit to get in the front beside her while her son was to sit forward from the back seat and hold Rabbit's shoulders so he could not move. His hands had already been tied behind his back.

At the station, a couple of policemen were outside talking to one another and they were asked to please assist in taking Rabbit inside, but he no longer gave them any resistance.

Rabbit clammed his mouth shut and refused to talk to the detective who finally said in a calm voice, "Look son. We aren't going to hurt you. We think you may have information that will help Colleen. We are not going to accuse you of anything."

"I'm black sir. I ain't no fool."

"Do you know that a black person at your school said the exact same thing. Why would you think we'd accuse you of being a fool?"

"Because I am black, and they will all say I killed Margie."

"Did you?"

"NO, I did not."

"Then you have nothing to worry about."

"Yes, I do. After I tell you what really happened, you will say I murdered

Margie."

"Do you think that just because you are black?"

"I don't THINK you will do that; I knows it."

"Ok, son, let's just see what happens after you tell us what happened?"

"I ain't your son. I never seen my father."

"I apologize."

They sat in the room another twenty or so minutes without either one saying anything. The detective got up to leave the room.

"Where you goin?"

"It's none of your business. If you won't talk to me, why should I talk to you?" The detective slammed the door on his way out.

Rabbit could not have been more stubborn. He just sat in the room, put his arms and head on the table, and he actually fell asleep. They let him sleep while they decided what they should do. Then one of the policemen said that maybe Roy should be called in to talk to him.

30

Some officers were sent over to Roy's house to see if he would come to the jail and talk to Rabbit. The father saw the police car and immediately intercepted them at the door before either one could knock. He was somewhat worried that because they went to the police, they had created more of a fiasco than planned, and maybe now the police thought in some way Roy was responsible for Margaret's death. The father spoke softly when he said, "What's up, and why are you here?"

One of the officers responded, "We have Rabbit at the jail, but he won't tell us anything. In fact, he fell asleep in the interrogation room."

"And, so?"

"The detective thought that maybe Roy might be able to get Rabbit to say something."

The father stood there in a daze wondering what to do. At that time, both Roy and his mother came into the living room from the kitchen mostly to see who was doing all the talking.

Finally, the father invited the two officers inside the home and offered them a seat. Both the men refused the seat and just stood there.

"Roy," said the father, "Rabbit's at the police station and the police detective thought maybe Rabbit might feel better talking with you present."

Without giving it much thought, Roy said he would be happy to go and try to get Rabbit to talk.

His mother, however, had other ideas. "You are not going anyplace unless your Dad and I can come too."

"Oh, sure you can both go," said the quiet cop.

The other cop gave him the evil eye, but he reneged when he realized if they wanted Roy it would be a package deal that included his mother and father.

"Can I ride in the police car Mom, please?"

"Well, we'll be following right behind you in our car, and we don't want you to say a word until we are seated beside you."

Roy's mother was chatty Cathy on the ride to the jail. While she wondered everything, she spoke out loud to her husband who was a nervous wreck. If he had his way, they would have remained silent.

"I wonder if this trip is going to be a consequence on our son in any way. I wonder if Rabbit is going to tell the same story he told Roy."

While the father wanted to tell his wife to "shut-up", he quietly said to his wife, "Honey, we won't know anything until we get there. It is just a short ride, so why don't we wait and see what happens."

"You mean you are not worried about what could happen?"

"I'm worried of course, but worrying doesn't solve anything."

At this point they were in eye's view of the jail, so no more was said by either parent.

Inside, they all peered into the window that showed Rabbit. He had recently awakened and was becoming fidgety.

The detective looked at Roy's parents and said, "I will go in with Roy. The rest of you are going to have to stay behind."

Roy's Mom started to object, but the father grabbed her hand and squeezed it so hard the mother quickly got the message she was not to intervene.

"You can stay and look in the window. While you can't hear what is being said, you will immediately know if something goes wrong when or if these two policemen enter the room."

Rabbit looked up when the Chief walked in with Roy. He shook his head negatively as though his friend had betrayed him.

The Chief said, "Your friend Roy came to visit you."

Rabbit shrugged and said nothing.

Roy attempted to engage him, but Rabbit, who was usually very loquacious, said absolutely nothing.

Finally, Roy got angry. He almost shouted, "You are the most selfish person I've ever met. You think mostly of yourself while giving no consideration to beautiful Colleen. She might go to prison because you choose to be quiet, and because you are too stupid to realize this fact."

That did arise some ire in Rabbit when he said, "Don't call me stupid."

The Detective was not expecting to hear that outburst come out of Roy's mouth, and he momentarily wondered if he had done the right thing by getting Roy to come and see Rabbit.

Roy continued, "I will continue to call you stupid if you keep acting in a stupid manner. I've already told the police why you were in the woods that day. You had no way of knowing that Colleen and Margie got in a fight in the girls' room."

"Yea, it's because of you the police came after me."

"So what? They are thinking you can help Colleen."

"Yea, they'll help her ok by blaming me for Margie's murder. And besides, she wasn't even murdered."

The Chief of Police snapped to attention at that statement, and with a tilt of his head urged Roy to continue the conversation.

"You say you know for sure Margie wasn't murdered?" Roy was pleased his conversation was yielding some results.

"No, she wasn't. I already told you that."

"Well, how did Margie die?"

"We both scared each other when we came to the area around a very large bush. Margie tripped on something and fell backwards hitting her head." Realizing he had just told the whole story, Rabbit got angry at Roy again. "You see what you made me do?"

"No, I don't as a matter of fact. What did I make you do?"

"I just yelled out everything that happened." Rabbit looked at the detective and said, "Well, what are you waiting for? Arrest me."

"Why should I arrest you son? Oh, I'm sorry, I should not have called you son. The way I see it, your story confirms what the janitor at the school said. I have no reason to arrest you."

Roy's mother realized there were two strangers also looking in the window. No one was telling the young man and a lady, who could have been his mother, to move, and she wondered why they were there.

The woman noticed Roy's mother staring at her and walked up and introduced herself.

"We all wondered where Rabbit had gone when he disappeared."

"Well, he really didn't disappear. He just came to visit us. He does this often during the summer months. We live in Keystone, the next town adjacent to this one. We had no idea the police were looking for Rabbit until my son heard the news through the grape vine."

"Did Rabbit volunteer to come?"

"Quite the contrary. We had to sort of force him. He was really reluctant to come."

At that point, they could all see the detective give those who were watching through the window a thumbs up. For the first time that evening, Roy's Dad heaved a sigh of relief.

The woman said to Roy's Mom, "It looks like your son got Rabbit to talk. Bravo to him."

"I hope they realize Rabbit did not hurt Margie, and I certainly hope they don't arrest him."

Hearing this statement, the son said, "Why should they arrest Rabbit? He didn't do anything wrong."

"I know, but he is black, and sometimes people are blamed just for their color."

"Well, they don't come any whiter than Colleen, and they had no problem arresting her either."

"I know, I know. Apparently, someone saw Colleen and Margie fighting though. Rabbit just happened to run into Margie by accident."

Roy's father joined the conversation at that point and said, "Maybe now that the truth is out, Colleen will be free, and everyone will know Margie's death was an accident. It does go to show you that just because two people are having a little tiff doesn't mean they will go and murder them."

The detective came out of the interrogation room and asked both the mother of the Keystone boy, and Roy's parents, if Rabbit could stay with them that evening. "Whoever says yes though will have to have Rabbit back here early in the morning. Once we can get in touch with Judge Stallone, I'll be bringing Rabbit to court along with the janitor tomorrow some time."

"Since he's already been staying with us and has some of his things at our home, I'll be happy to take Rabbit home and bring him back here early tomorrow morning."

Roy's mother wanted to say they had some of Rabbit's things at their home too, but in retrospect she felt that Roy needed his sleep. If they were to take Rabbit to their home tonight, she feared the two boys would be up all night talking. So, she was happy she did not have to volunteer to take him and was grateful someone else had done so.

31

Doris was pouring herself a cup of coffee when the phone rang. She glanced at the clock on the wall. It only said 7:30 a.m., and she wondered who would be calling them so early in the morning. She shuffled over to the phone in her comfy slippers and said, "Hello."

It was their attorney saying that some new evidence had been brought to the police department's attention, and they all were to be in court today by 10:00 that morning. "However, could you please be in that private room at the courthouse by 9:00? I haven't heard this new evidence, but I want to be sure none of us is late."

When Jack heard his wife say, yes, we'll be there, he mouthed the words without making a sound as he inquired who was on the phone. The frown on Jack's face confirmed he was asking a question. At that point though, Doris had placed the phone on the receiver, so Jack knew the call had been completed.

"We have to be at court at 9 o'clock this morning. I'll explain later."

"I had better run to the bar and tell them I won't be available today. I also have to change into a suit."

"I'm going to go find your mother. I would imagine she will want to go and see what the heck is happening." Doris found Jack's mother making her bed in her room. Used to getting up early she was already dressed for the day, but she decided to wear something more fitting for the courtroom. Though, they really did not know if this were going to be a real court day, or not.

At the other end of town in the hotel, the Chapmans had just ordered room service and were getting ready to eat when their hotel phone rang. The same conversation happened as at the O'Conner's house, only the Chapmans were more suspicious. "Maybe the O'Conner family decided to take a settlement."

"I always thought the money would be too good to turn down."

"Well, we don't have too much time to get ready. We can talk in the car later," said Mr. Chapman.

The two couples passed each other in the courtroom hallway. They both just nodded an acknowledgment to each other and kept on walking in opposite directions.

Tom was already in the room when the three members of the O'Conner family walked in. The lawyer shook their hands and offered all three a seat as he scrambled around to get more available chairs.

"What's up?" Jack was the first one to speak.

"I'm afraid I have nothing to tell you this morning. We were not given any information with the exception to say that the police have more evidence."

Doris spoke up wondering if that was good news or bad news.

"I wish I had more to tell you. Honestly, I just don't know. If you can bear with me, we should all know close to the ten o'clock hour."

Jack just had a terrible feeling of remorse. At this point in the trial, nothing was good as far as he was concerned.

They were offered some coffee, juice or water, but none of them cared for anything. For one thing, they were concerned about getting in the courtroom and then having to use the rest room. For another reason, they were all just too nervous at this point.

When they entered the courtroom, it was an eerie feeling. The room was mostly empty. They saw the Chapmans seated by their lawyer and they were approaching their seats near their own attorney. Silence filled the room when they noticed Colleen being escorted to a seat. Her hair was a tangle of curls though the curls appeared to have been brushed and in actuality, Colleen looked stunning despite the anguish that she felt.

The two attorneys were asked to approach the bench after Judge Stallone entered the room. The lawyers seemed intense as the Judge spoke to them, with the Chapman's attorney asking the most questions, except no one could hear what was being said. When they returned to their seats both talked to their clients. Tom got the attention of the three O'Conner family members when he said, "It's good news."

He was bombarded with questions from all three of them, but at that time the Judge immediately called the court to order.

Everyone straightened in their seats and looked at the Judge without making a sound. What on earth was he going to say?

"May I have your attention Ladies and Gentlemen. Some evidence has been brought to this court that confirms that Margaret Chapman's death was an accident. She was not murdered. We have two eyewitnesses that confirm her death was an accident. Neither one of them has been in contact with the other from what we can determine."

There was a lot of commotion coming from the Chapmans' area and the room was filled with gasps at the Judge's statement. The O'Conner family still had not completely digested what was being said. Of course, they wondered how this information was going to impact their daughter. Sitting between her husband and mother, Doris quickly grabbed her husband's hand and did the same with Cora. Both squeezed her hands tightly and held on like she might run away.

The Judge continued, "You all may wonder why these witnesses did not mention what they saw sooner. At this point I can only say their reasons were valid and all of you will be getting a copy of the complete report that will explain everything to you. Of course, your attorneys will also keep you informed. This has all been verified with the police and the coroner has checked the body and confirms his original statement that it appears to have been an accident. However, after hearing testimony from the junior varsity girl cheerleaders in court that they heard Colleen and Margie arguing, no one was sure. It is obvious that someone botched this investigation crudely, and the powers that be were too willing to accuse an innocent person.

Believe me, that matter will be further examined and those responsible will be apprehended accordingly."

Taking a sip of water out of a glass on his desk, the Judge temporarily stopped talking. When he continued, he changed his position and looked in the direction of Colleen. "Young lady," he said, "you have been a model prisoner. You never complained, and you respected our rules even though you knew you did not commit a crime. You are to be commended for your behavior."

Colleen looked at the Judge with her big eyes wondering what all this meant. The Judge finally said, "Miss Colleen O'Conner, you have been acquitted and are free to go."

No one moved. It was as though they did not comprehend what had just been said. Then Mr. Wagner said to Doris, "Go, hug your daughter. She is free to go home with you today. One of you can stop by tomorrow to pick up what little belongings your daughter had while in jail. Today, I am sure you just want to take her home and digest all that has transpired."

Doris nearly ran from her seat and grabbed her daughter giving her the biggest bear hug ever. The father and the grandmother soon followed and did the same as Doris by hugging and kissing the child.

Confusion was on the minds of the Chapmans. They still could not grasp the obvious. Colleen looked in their direction and asked her parents to please excuse her for a minute. She was gone before they could stop her. She ran over to the Chapmans and gave Mrs. Chapman a quick hug while saying, "Mrs. Chapman, I want you to know that Margie was a friend of mine. I would never even think of harming her. Her death has filled me with great sorrow, and I am happy to know that no one else harmed Margie either. I know it probably doesn't matter to you what I think, since your daughter will be dead either way. I am sorry for your loss." She shook Mr. Chapman's hand and quickly walked back to her parents without giving the Chapmans a chance to respond.

At that, with Colleen still dressed in her jail room attire, the members of the O'Conner family walked out of the courtroom to their car with their heads held high. To say they were happy would be an understatement. Their minds were still filled with all kinds of questions, but those would be answered soon enough. Today they were bringing their daughter home, and all was good with the world.

32

Little Johnny, who lived down the street from Colleen, was the local paper boy. He would awaken in the wee hours of the morning, grab his bundles of newspapers that had been left in a hidden area on his front porch, assemble them individually and ride his bike while flinging the newspapers into the yards of his customers. Johnny had a secret crush on Colleen thinking there was no one more beautiful in the world. He intended to marry Colleen once he had grown into adulthood. He gave no consideration to the fact that Colleen would have also grown that much more too. He had a goal, and as far as he was concerned, he was going to achieve it.

Seeing the headline in the newspaper, Johnny immediately got an idea from watching the newsreels at the local movie theater. After delivering all his daily newspapers, he rode his bike to the Journal office and asked if he could have a bundle of extra papers from today. This was not a normal request, but Johnny was a favorite of the newsroom staff and they gave him a bundle just out of curiosity to see what Johnny intended to do. Johnny rode to the business part of Main Boulevard and putting his bike on the ground, he grabbed one of the papers and shouted, "Extra, Extra, read all about it. Beautiful Colleen is free." People scooped up the papers like wildfire, and Johnny kept biking back to the Journal building for more newspapers.

The people in the newsroom were beside themselves with awe. They sold more newspapers that day than ever before. Johnny loved his job once he got up in the morning. Getting up early was one of the worst parts of the job, but once awakened he loved riding his bike around town and throwing the papers into people's yards. He was becoming quite skilled when he tossed the papers, so that most of the papers landed near his customers' front doors. The only thing he did not like was the day of the week where he had to ask for money. Most of the people were kind, and Johnny got good tips, but there were a few kooks who refused to answer their door even though he knew they were at home. There was the lady who lived alone and always answered the door in the nude. Johnny tried so hard not to look at all her parts, but being ten years old, it was hard. His parents had always told him not to enter anyone's home, so when the lady invited him in, he always tactfully refused. One thing to her credit was that she always paid, and gave him a generous tip. Johnny also had a deep recognition of what he should say to his parents and what he shouldn't say. He instinctively knew enough not to mention any customers state of dress or non-dress to the parents ever. That was a number one no-no.

At the end of the day, Johnny was absolutely thrilled with the stash of money he made and could not wait to get home and show his parents. Another plus was that his beautiful Colleen would be back at the house and he could idolize her from his home once again.

33

Doris, Jack and Cora were not prepared to have a normal celebration in their home at the homecoming of their daughter. This was not only awkward, but a distraction. The O'Conner family entered the house and then appeared to be at a loss as to what to do next. It was like after a stay as an inpatient in a hospital. You were happy to be home, but you also did not know you would be home, so everything seemed disoriented. They kind of all were in shock and stared at each other hoping some miracle would occur to make them happy. Yet, in reality, the miracle had already happened. The family was just not ready.

All had heard the news of why Colleen was free to go home, but the information had yet to register in their brains. Prepared for a long, drawn out trial, none of them could quite comprehend what they were supposed to do now. Finally, Grandma said, "I'm going to prepare a favorite meal tonight for you honey. Just tell me what you would like, and voila!"

Colleen thought for a long time until they almost feared she wasn't going to speak. Then her sweet voice said, "I'm trying to decide what I would prefer. On the one hand I want spaghetti in homemade tomato sauce, meatballs and sausage with a salad, but on the other hand I want pot roast with veggies and egg noodles."

"Well, decide no more honey. You shall have both. I'll just change my clothes to something more comfortable and run out to the store to get the ingredients. Also, I'll make your favorite dessert – lemon meringue pie."

Both Doris and Colleen walked up to Jack's Mother and gave her a huge hug. "Sounds perfect, Ma." It had taken Doris many weeks to feel comfortable calling her mother-in-law Ma or Mom, but she was such a gracious, kind person, that it became easier with time. Now, it just seemed right and natural to do so.

"If you don't mind, I think I'll go up to my room and call my friends."

"That's a great idea honey," said Doris. "I have some paperwork that I can do for the store anyway, and it might as well get done sooner rather than later."

Colleen ran upstairs and while she did so, Doris mentally thought to herself that she wished she had decorated the house in some special Homecoming way, but they really did not have the time, nor did they have the energy to do otherwise. Yes, Colleen's room had been cleaned spotless every day. Not that it ever got dirty, but they cleaned it more to have something to do. Besides, being around Colleen's "stuff" somehow made all of them feel better.

Barbara answered the phone and was so excited to hear her friend's voice. "Where are you? Wait a minute, Mia is here. I'll call her to get near the phone so we can both hear you."

"What a marvelous surprise," said Mia.

"I'm home, and I'm free. Isn't that wonderful?"

"Oh, wow, tell us what happened?"

"It's a long story, if you have the time."

"We'll make the time."

"I got a lot of the information from your Dad, Mia, before we left the courtroom. I'll tell you as much as I know until we get further information."

Colleen proceeded to tell the story and her friends were flabbergasted.

Mia interjected, "If Rabbit knew all along, why didn't he say something? My God, the way those girls testified that you and Margie were having a fight, I almost was beginning to believe them, even though I knew in my heart it could not be true. They were junior varsity cheerleaders, but cheerleaders usually stick together with their varsity friends. Some friends they turned out to be. Rabbit should have said something from the beginning."

"That's easy for us to say Mia. As hard as it is to understand, I somehow think I do comprehend why not only Rabbit would do such a thing, but the school janitor as well."

"He saw it too?" Barbara was disbelieving. "Why would they do such a thing. In some people's minds your reputation is going to be ruined forever."

"I know," was Colleen's response, "but I've already forgiven them. They both were terrified."

"Terrified of what," interrupted Mia, "it was your character that was slandered."

"We have to put our positions in their place to understand."

"They saw someone trip and fall and die from it. What's to understand?"

"Well, we are not colored, so maybe we'll never know their fear."

"Is that what made them so afraid, because they were colored?"

"Yes, they both said the same thing, and they had never talked to each other about it."

"My God, that's awful that people are afraid just because they are of a different race."

"Well, the police and the Judge assured them that in this case they have nothing to fear. So, in the end everything will be alright."

"Why were you fighting with Margie anyway? That is so unlike you." Barbara still appeared to be somewhat in shock.

"It was a personal matter between Margie and me. I'd rather not ever discuss it."

"Well, if that's the way you want to be. Remember though, we've never kept a secret from any one of us, so I don't know why we should start now when the case is over." Mia sounded really irritated.

"Let's put it this way. I don't feel like talking about it now, but most likely I will mention it to you some day."

Barbara, the practical one settled the whole thing when she said, "That's fine with us. The decision is yours and we'll abide by it." She said this while giving her friend a jab in the side to reiterate her message. The subject was dropped, and they finally went on to other things.

By then, Colleen realized she had been on the phone for ages. She said her goodbyes as the aroma from the kitchen teased her nose. Upon hanging the phone on the receiver, she ran down to the kitchen while saying, "I haven't smelled anything this good in ages."

The mood in the family had gotten somewhat back to normal. Knowing this, the party was about to begin.

34

It did not matter that there was proof that Colleen was innocent. There would always be an element of society that chose to believe she was guilty. Who knows why they felt this way? Perhaps it was out of envy not only of Colleen's beauty, but the envy also of her good-looking family that adored her, or the fact they owned a lively business – two businesses actually with the convenience store and the bar. Maybe they wanted to believe that no one could be that nice and kind.

Reprimands to individuals involved in the court case ran high in the courthouse community. The Janitor and Rabbit both got off easy because of a compassionate Judge Stallone. This town in the lower northeastern states in the 1950's was basically friendly to all races and some of the schools were integrated with no one being left out because of religion or color. As a small town, everyone in that area was fortunate in that regard. Yet, the Judge could understand the fears of both colored men having been around long enough to comprehend what their histories endured. The Prosecuting Attorneys were prohibited from trying any murder cases for six months. This appeared odd and ludicrous since there were not a lot of murders committed in the town. The Judge felt the prosecutors were quick to rush to judgment and accuse Colleen of murder. He found this to be preposterous and a poor choice. The verbal scolding given by the Judge was enough to make anyone cringe.

College admissions were arriving every day in the mail. Barbara and Mia both would be attending schools on the east coast. Colleen, though she had also been accepted at an east coast university, was still undecided as to what she should do. The time spent in jail, and the horrible accusations against her, made their mark on her normal cheerful personality.

On a lovely summer evening in August, everyone in the O'Conner family sat in their backyard enjoying the unusually pleasant temperatures. Cora became the focus of attention when she remarked, "I've been doing a lot of thinking lately. I would like your opinion on my thoughts."

Everyone glanced her way waiting for her to say more. "I need to go back to Missouri and decide what to do with the house. I left rather quickly to come east when I heard the unfortunate news."

"We want you to continue to live with us Ma," said her son.

"I do like it here and will probably move back someday to be near all of you. I never realized I missed the east coast so much. Living so close to the ocean, it is not uncommon here to get a whiff of sea air on occasion. Yet, a few miles in the opposite direction are beautiful mountains. Frankly, the consistency of tornado warnings where I now live have always frightened me. What I would like to do is take Colleen back to Missouri with me. I live near a college town and there is a Junior College and a University within close distance. The Junior College will definitely take Colleen, and I feel she needs to get away from this area for a while. My home is certainly big enough, and Colleen can fix one of the bedrooms any way she wants. In four years, we will both return east."

Doris and Jack were not so sure of this proposal as a sad look covered both their faces. How could they let their only child travel so far away?

Cora snapped to attention immediately when she saw the sad look on both their faces by saying, "I know this comes as a shock to you both right now as we have never even considered such a proposition. Knowing this, take your time deciding what would be best. I'll go along with whatever you decide."

What surprised everyone was when Colleen jumped out of her chair, grabbing her grandmother and twirling her around. "Grandma, you have made my day. I would love to go to school in the Midwest and come and live with you. Frankly, I've been so worried about staying in this area right now. I get this awful feeling everyone is staring at me. In Missouri, I'll just be another member of the crowd."

Colleen looked at the faces of both her mother and father and quickly said, "You both can come and visit us, Mom and Dad. Think of how great that would be."

Doris and Jack tried to look happy, but the extreme loss they both felt in their hearts held them back.

"We'll work it out darling."

Running up the stairs, Colleen shouted she was going to call her friends and tell them. In her mind, it was a done deal.

"Think about it," said Cora. "I'm going up to bed now. We all have a lot to consider.

Jack and Doris remained in the unlit backyard. The evening was still beautiful. For a while, they sat on the swing watching the activity of some lightening bugs as they created a dichotomy of interspersed light flashing intermittently in the darkened atmosphere. Jack looked at his wife and finally said, "I bet you were as beautiful when you were young as you are right now."

All of a sudden, Doris felt a little frisky as she said, "You bet your bottom dollar I was."

Jack enveloped his wife in his arms and gave her an extremely passionate kiss. "Let's go upstairs," he said.

"Gladly," said Doris. "Thank God we've got such a wonderful family. We'll get through this the same way we always get through other obstacles in our lives."

At that, John picked up his wife hoping to carry her up the stairs, but he soon sat her back down. "We may be too old for some things, he said, but certainly not for others." They both laughed as they rushed upstairs.

35

Jack had maps sprawled all over the kitchen table the next day. The decision had been made, and he was already planning a trip to Missouri. "Shall we drive or take the train?"

Doris thought for a moment then decided, "Why don't we drive. That way we can stop and see some special sights along the way. Who knows, but maybe in the future I'll be brave enough to take one of those airplanes to get there quicker. If we do so, it will be for special occasions. That's after we drive the first time." She leaned over the kitchen table as they both checked the route on the maps and decided where they would stop along the way.

The Grandmother and Colleen were also making their plans. Colleen had attempted to pack some suitcases already, but she was taking so many things she was having a hard time getting them shut.

Finally, Cora said to her granddaughter when she saw the stuffed suitcases, "We do have stores in Missouri dear. What you don't take with you we can certainly buy there."

There was a knock on the back screen-door. Since most people they knew came to the front door, Jack and Doris looked at each other in wonderment as did Colleen and her grandmother upstairs in Colleen's room. Jack left the map scattered across the kitchen table to see who was knocking. He could hear voices but could not make them out. Jack was surprised to see the school janitor, Rabbit and Roy standing there. They all had nicely pressed cotton shirts on with clean long pants which they later found out had been purchased and pressed by the janitor's wife. Without a moment's hesitation, Jack invited the three into his home.

Each of the three had a nicely wrapped gift which they later explained they were giving to Colleen. One had a box of candy, another some small jarred home-made jellies, and there was also a basket of fresh fruit with a big bow tied around the handle. Doris offered them something to drink and had them sit in the living room where she placed a plate of cookies on the coffee table. Jack had already yelled up the stairs for Colleen and Cora to come down. Since they were both curious who would be coming to the back of their house, Jack did not have to call them twice.

The smile on Colleen's face when she saw the three "musketeers" as she later called them, melted their hearts. Colleen was unaware that people also used the same phrase for her own group of gal friends. The original musketeers' motto seemed equally fitting for the three girls - "All for one, and one for all, united we stand, divided we fall".

"We so happy to see you Miss Colleen," said the janitor. "We come to apologize for our bad behavior." One could tell he had been practicing what to say.

"Yea," said Rabbit, "We so sorry you had to go to jail. We should have said something sooner, but we was so scared."

Roy just sat there agreeing with everything they said.

"I'm happy to now be home," expressed Colleen. "I know you meant no harm. That's all over now. I don't want you to worry about it anymore."

They approached Colleen one at a time, each giving her a gift and a big hug.

"You were all very kind to come here to apologize. These gifts are wonderful. Thank you so much, plus you all look very sharp in your nicely pressed outfits."

They all got a shy smile on their faces, and Roy said, "We can thank the janitor's wife for getting us these shirts and pants, pressing them, and making us look so sharp." He stood up and straightened his shoulders as though to make himself look even better. The other two that accompanied Roy imitated his actions.

After a little more small-talk, and when their drinks were finished, the three readied themselves to leave.

Colleen restated how appreciative she was of their visit and saw them to the front door. All the family followed the three to the door to say their goodbyes.

"Well, I'll be damned," said Jack after the guys left. "That was downright classy of them to do that."

* * *

Today was the day Colleen and her grandmother were going to the city. They planned to buy a few things, see a show, and eat at a Chinese Restaurant of which there were none in their small town. They hopped a train early having already purchased their show tickets. It was going to be a leisurely day with no rushing around. The grandmother did not know that Colleen also had other plans until they stopped at a deli for some breakfast.

"I hope you don't mind Grandma, but I am going to meet with Margie's parents later this morning. There is something I want to say to them before I leave the area."

"Are you going to tell me what it is?"

"Sorry Grandma, but this is just between the family and myself."

"Then, I won't push you any more to know what it is. What will I do, when you are talking with the Chapmans?"

"They know you will be with me. I won't be long."

"Honestly, I really don't want to see them. I'll wait in the lobby for you."

"I'll notify them of this when I give them a phone call before we get a taxi."

Secretly, the Grandmother could not help but wonder if the conversation concerned the reason why Colleen became so closed mouth every time she was asked about the fight between Margie and herself. It did not matter to her either way, to be frank. What was done, was done. Her Colleen was home now, and that is all that mattered to her.

"What time are we going there dear?"

"At 11:30 this morning. They wanted us to stay for lunch, but while I thanked them, I said our schedule was too tight."

"It was hard enough to lose your grandfather. I can't imagine what they are feeling having lost a daughter. That is not to mention all the drama that followed her death."

"I still can't believe it all, Grandma. Staying in jail was a nightmare."

"I know honey. I can get nightmares just thinking about you being there."

They both left the coffee shop, did some errands, and Colleen found a phone booth to make her call to the Chapman's before 11:00 a.m. when they hailed a taxi.

36

The Chapmans were sitting in their living room with its elegant furnishings. The interior of their apartment defied the décor of the hotel. Everything was ultra-modern in various shades of white. Brightly tinted throw pillows added touches of color to offset the white. The couches were of white leather and very plush. Everything in the room exuded money from the buffet to the expensive items displayed around the room. Some were modern style Lladro figurines that were distinctive in their style, while others appeared to be luxurious as though made especially for the Chapmans by their own personal artist or sculptor. Fresh flowers were placed tastefully around the room, their vases radiating a monetary influence. Their apartment was located in the penthouse, and until central air conditioning became in vogue, they often opened the windows. Classic Custom Roller shades were appropriately placed in all the windows. The Chapmans were fortunate as they did not get the hot afternoon sun, and they overlooked the immaculately kept park.

In a stupor, the parents, for the life of them, could not figure out why Colleen was visiting them. "It's over now. Our daughter is still dead. They said it was an accident, and Colleen was set free. So why is she coming to see us?" Mrs. Chapman was beside herself with concern.

"I've been wondering the same thing, honey. Honestly, I still think someone killed our daughter. What they described as her behavior makes absolutely no sense. She was not the kind to go around mumbling to herself. And, in the woods yet."

"What do you suppose the two girls were having a fight about?"

"For the life of me, I just don't know. Probably a boy they both liked."

"While I do think someone murdered our daughter, I really don't think Colleen would do such a thing, but maybe she had that Rabbit kid do it for her."

"Now you're stretching it hon. Kids don't think that way. They are not from this city where we hear this kind of stuff all the time. People who do these things are usually adults though and not children, and they pay large sums of money to have someone do the killing for them. Those from the small town are individuals who think in small town ways. Most of them don't have that kind of money."

"I suppose. I was rather shocked when she came over to us at the jail. It was nice of her to do that, however. Her parents seemed just as shocked as we were."

"Well her phone call indicated they are on the way, so it's almost time for her to get here. We'll know soon enough. I feel funny though having her grandmother remain in the lobby, but apparently that is her choice."

* * *

Both the grandmother's eyes, as well as the eyes of Colleen, nearly popped out of their heads when the taxi pulled up in front of the apartment complex. Neither had ever seen anything so elegant. The lawn and bushes were well manicured and brightly colored flowers were interspersed throughout the grounds in all the right places. Two huge lion statues were at the head of the canopied walkway entrance to the building.

A doorman dressed in black pants and a red jacket with gold buttons over a white shirt opened the taxi door after the grandmother paid and tipped the driver. The hat on the doorman's head was shaped like a cap with a visor. In the middle of the cloth part of the cap was an emblem with the apartment complex's signature letters. He escorted the two females into the lobby area which was filled with brightly colored plush chairs and couches. Each area was decorated as though it were an individual living room area that would accommodate around five people. The purpose obviously indicated that one could gather in an area and enjoy a private conversation without disturbing someone else. Each separate place had either a round or rectangular mahogany coffee table placed on oriental throw rugs over the highly polished wooden floors, and smaller mahogany end tables were placed beside each chair or couch.

The grandmother made a circle with her thumb and pointy finger to indicate she would be okay with her accommodations while waiting. Colleen had pushed the letter P for penthouse on the special elevator that had been shown to her by the receptionist. The interior of the elevator was covered in mirrors where Colleen practiced different facial expressions she might use. In reality, she would not have been concerned with what her face did if she were just in an ordinary elevator. So, as she exited the elevator, for the first time that day Colleen began to feel somewhat anxious.

The butler answered the door and escorted her to both Chapmans, and they stood to greet her.

As they stood, Colleen could not help but notice how stylish Mrs. Chapman looked, and it appeared to be effortless though it most likely was not. Her ecru silk slacks and dark brown silk shirt highlighted her bleached blonde locks. Mr. Chapman had on a stylish fashionable smoking jacket also made of silk and the burgundy color highlighted his tanned skin creating the look of a movie star. Even though smoking jackets were normally worn in the evening, or after dinner, Mr. Chapman knew he would be smoking and found the jacket to be comfortable leisure wear that kept his other clothes underneath from smelling too smoky. They shook Colleen's hand and offered her a seat. The butler had already placed some pastries on the dining room buffet with coffee or tea and offered to bring both to Colleen who accepted. Colleen took them not because she was hungry, but she felt it would be rude if she refused.

Nor did Colleen beat around the bush, but this young woman got right to the point of why she came to visit the Chapmans that day.

"I wanted you to know that contrary to what the junior varsity cheerleaders said, Margie and I were not having a fight. I'm hoping you know your daughter's sexual preference. I believe Margie misinterpreted my kindness to her as misguided affection, and she grabbed me as though she were going to hug and kiss me. At first, I thought she was going to remove something like a bug off my blouse. When I felt her coming closer, I pushed her away. Though, when I pushed her it was not in anger but more out of confusion, as I just had no idea at the time what was occurring. I was more frustrated with myself. I felt I had given Margie the wrong impression. The cheerleaders walked in the girls' room at exactly that moment. I never had a real chance to explain to Margie that I don't kiss girls, but that I certainly did not judge her for what she felt."

Mrs. Chapman remained speechless, and so did her husband for some minutes. He then said, "We think Margie was confused. This is not normal for us."

Colleen then became speechless.

"Did you tell anyone about what happened?" This was the concern of Margie's mother.

"No Mam, I did not. I did not even tell my attorney who told me he could sense that something bothered me. He also said, if I did not tell him, I was most likely going to be convicted of murder. This is all so new to me, but if I knew anything, I knew I could not tell what happened. And, anyway, who would believe me?"

"Thank you for your concern about our daughter's welfare."

"I can't stay much longer. My grandmother and I have a busy time planned, and I am going to school in Missouri. The need for me is great to just get away from the east coast for a while. It has been a traumatic few months. I just wanted you to know that I liked Margie a lot. I would never murder her. I hope you can understand that. Thank you for seeing me. I appreciate your candor. I am extremely sorry at the loss of Margie. I know how I feel, and I cannot really imagine what it is like to lose your only daughter. Again, thank you. I'll let myself out."

Both parents stood there in shock. Colleen was gone before they even said their proper goodbyes. The mother would never in her lifetime believe their daughter was "gay". Frankly, they just did not understand the entire situation. Months later, they were comforted by Colleen's words. They appreciated the fact that she did not tell anyone what their daughter did to her that day. Their family had a secret, and that secret would never be revealed to anyone as long as they lived.

Cora was so excited to see her gorgeous granddaughter exit the elevator. She could not help but notice several people turn around to get a second look at her, both men and women.

"Sit here beside me dear, and tell me all about your visit. The clothes they wore, the décor of their place – everything. We still have time before going to the museum which is not too far from here. After, we can shop, and later we can go to our room, shower and dress to beat the band."

Colleen secretly loved her grandmother's expressions like beat the band, and yet somehow, she knew exactly what it meant.

"Just think," Cora continued, "When we are ready to leave here, the doorman will even hail a cab for us. I'm not going to turn that service away."

Colleen did sit down, more out of relief for what she had done, than anything else. Before the Grandmother knew it, Colleen started talking and didn't stop. Yet, she never revealed a word of what she had said to Margie's parents. She told about the elevator with the glass interior, the penthouse, the clothes worn by the Chapmans, the butler. "I'm so stuffed Grandma. I just could not refuse the pastries that were offered to me. It seemed I would be rude if I did so."

"I know the feeling honey, as I've done it many times myself when visiting people."

EPILOGUE

Colleen graduated from the University in Missouri. Doris, Jack and the Grandmother were all there to see her on her proud day. In fact, they were honored to be there. Colleen came back east and got a publishing job in the city for a big-name publisher. The drive to the city took about an hour from her parents. In later years she advocated for social justice issues like ageism, discrimination and homophobia. She married an attorney, had three children (two girls and a boy), and bought a home in one of the newer suburbs adjacent to the city where she continued to work.

Cora sold her home in Missouri and bought a small bungalow in an adjoining town next to Doris and Jack. She adored being back on the east coast near her son and wife and visited them often. Enamored at being a great grandmother, Cora was beside herself when Colleen had her own children.

Barbara became a physician specializing in obstetrics. She never married. Early in her senior year in high school, her boyfriend was killed in a car crash. She was fortunate to be able to adopt a boy and a girl who were brother and sister from a source still unknown. Adoption was not normally granted to a single woman during that time period. For years Barbara worked with her Dad while training to be a specialist. When her Dad retired, he left the practice to her. It pretty much included the waiting area and exam rooms, plus some equipment, as his was a practice for a general practitioner. With some remodeling, Barbara was easily able to practice obstetrics and gynecology and the parents lived in their own apartment attached to the original larger home. Barbara continued to live in the main house.

Mia also married an attorney whom she met after college, when as a young man, he went to work for the same group as Mia's Dad. Together they had two boys and two girls. Barbara was her OB/GYN doctor. They purchased a home in one of the newer townships near her hometown. She became a high-ranking civil service employee at the nearby Fort.

Rabbit's mother took off for parts unknown and was never seen again. Years later there was speculation she probably died from a drug overdose. The Janitor and his wife immediately took Rabbit under their wings. Both the Janitor and Rabbit thought alike. Home life suited Rabbit. He and Roy went to the same vocational school and joined together in a plumbing practice. Rabbit never married and purchased a lovely new one-bedroom apartment. Roy married a girl he met in high school. In their huge home in the suburbs they raised one child – a darling little girl that they called Princess. She was the icing on the cake as far as Roy's parents were concerned.

Doris and Jack eventually sold their home, convenience store and bar to an excited buyer. They bought a lovely bungalow down the street from Cora.

The newspaper boy gave up his love affair with beautiful Irish Colleen when a cute little Italian girl moved into the house next door to his. He loved going to her house for the delicious food that was always in abundance there. Besides, she was curved in all the right places. They went on to have an abundance of children and were considered to be model Catholics by their church.

A M E N